Joyfully Uplifting Ourselves and Others

How to Lead Effectively in Early Childhood Education

by

Teresa A. Byington, Ph.D.
Professor Emerita
University of Nevada
Reno Extension

Geraldine "Gigi" Wynn M.A.
University of Nevada
Reno Extension

Danielle C. Pertile, M.Ed.
University of Nevada
Reno Extension

Charmika "Mika" Hansen, M.Ed.
University of Nevada
Reno Extension

·P A U L·H·
BROOKES
PUBLISHING CO®

Baltimore • London • Sydney

·PAUL·H·
BROOKES
PUBLISHING CO®

Paul H. Brookes Publishing Co.
Post Office Box 10624
Baltimore, Maryland 21285-0624
USA
www.brookespublishing.com

Typeset by Westchester Publishing Services UK.
Manufactured in the United States of America by Versa Press, Inc., East Peoria, Illinois.

All examples in this book are composites. Any similarity to actual individuals or circumstances is coincidental, and no implications should be inferred.

The individuals described in this book are composites or real people whose situations are masked and are based on the authors' experiences. In all instances, names and identifying details have been changed to protect confidentiality.

Case studies are real people or composites based on the authors' experiences.
Real names and identifying details are used by permission.

Library of Congress Cataloging-in-Publication Control Number: 2026947311

ISBN 9781681259475 (paperback)
ISBN 9781681259482 (epub)
ISBN 9781681259499 (pdf)

British Library Cataloguing in Publication data are available from the British Library.

2031 2030 2029 2028 2027
10 9 8 7 6 5 4 3 2 1

Contents

About the Online Materials

Purchasers of this book may download, print, and/or photocopy Appendices for professional use.

To access the materials that come with this book:

1. Go to the Brookes Download Hub: http://downloads.brookespublishing.com.
2. Register to create an account (or log in with an existing account).
3. Filter or search for the book title *Joyfully Uplifting Ourselves and Others: How to Lead Effectively in Early Childhood Education.*

About the Authors

Teresa A. Byington, Ph.D., Professor Emerita, University of Nevada, Reno Extension

Dr. Teresa A. Byington was a joyful professor of early childhood education at the University of Nevada, Reno for 20 years. With years of experience as an educator, researcher, leader, and trainer across diverse educational sectors, she brings a wealth of knowledge and energy to her work. Teresa is the author of several books, including *Find the Joyful Leader Within* and *Lose the Lecture: Engaging Approaches to Early Childhood Professional Learning,* which focus on cultivating joyful leadership and dynamic professional learning practices. Her work celebrates the transformative power of joy in education and invites readers to reimagine how they can positively impact others.

Geraldine "Gigi" Wynn M.A. SPED., Early Childhood Education Coordinator, University of Nevada, Reno Extension

Geraldine "Gigi" Wynn is an inspiring early childhood education coordinator at the University of Nevada, Reno, where she supports and motivates the early childhood workforce through professional development, strength-based coaching sessions, and mentorship. With over 20 years of experience, she has worked as an early childhood teacher, assistant director, center director, QRIS coach, early childhood coach, leader, and professional development trainer across the United States. Gigi has transitioned from student to candidate as she continues pursuing her PhD in organizational development and leadership with an emphasis on training and e-learning. Her passion lies at the center of supporting people and is a beacon of light for all to be their best selves. She is also a proud wife, mom, and new "Nana Gigi."

Danielle C. Pertile, M.Ed., Early Childhood Education Coordinator, University of Nevada, Reno Extension

Danielle Pertile is an Early Childhood Education Coordinator at the University of Nevada, Reno Extension, where she leads the Spiral Up Academy training and coaching program designed to support and uplift new professionals entering the field of early childhood education. With over 20 years of experience, Danielle's career has included roles as a family camp counselor, nanny, toddler and preschool classroom teacher, early intervention developmental specialist, and now, trainer and coach. She holds a bachelor's degree in early childhood education and a master's degree in early childhood special education with an emphasis on infant/toddler development, both from the University of Nevada, Las Vegas. Danielle lives in Las Vegas with her husband, their son, and their dog, Watson.

Charmika "Mika" Hansen, M.Ed., Early Childhood Education Coordinator, University of Nevada, Reno Extension

Charmika "Mika" Hansen is an Early Childhood Education Coordinator with the University of Nevada, Reno Extension, where she has supported Nevada's early childhood workforce through coaching, mentoring, and dynamic professional development. With over 20 years of direct experience as a teacher, center director, trainer, community specialist, and training designer, Mika is passionate about uplifting educators and improving the quality of care and education for young children across Nevada. In her current role, Mika specializes in developing high-quality training content for online platforms, in-person workshops, and virtual learning sessions. She holds a master's degree in early childhood education and lives in Las Vegas with her son, daughter, and their goldendoodle. Mika's greatest joy is empowering others to grow, thrive, and create spaces where everyone feels valued and uplifted.

Acknowledgments

Writing this book has been a journey of learning, laughter, and deep reflection, and it would not have been possible without an incredible circle of support. We are deeply grateful to Cathyrn Peshlakai, Sarah Wright, Linda Logan, Miguel Pinedo, Michael Maxwell, Jenna Weglarz-Ward, Debbie Kaye, Orinthia Harris, and Mercedes Hutchins for their thoughtful feedback on our manuscript. Your insights helped shape this book into something far richer.

Special thanks to Robb Clouse and the editorial team at Brooks Publishing for all their expertise and steady support. We also extend our appreciation to the early childhood team at the University of Nevada, Reno Extension, whose collaboration and dedication have inspired us in countless ways. Additionally, we express sincere thanks to the many leaders in the early childhood field who have enriched our lives, shared their stories, and continue to make a joyful uplifting difference in the world. Thank you for lifting hearts, sparking hope, and showing the power of kindness in action. You are the true uplifters!

TERESA A. BYINGTON

I would like to thank my family, especially my husband Brad, for his love and support and my children for their patience and care. To my friends, I truly appreciate your kindness and words of encouragement. To my coauthors (Gigi, Danielle, and Mika), it has been a joy bringing this book to life. Your creativity and wealth of knowledge and experience are a gift that you freely give to others. Most of all, I value your friendship. Thank you for joining me in this joyful uplifting journey!

To the early childhood leaders who dedicate their hearts to children every day, thank you for your tireless commitment. As champions for children, you exemplify resilience and grace under pressure. I hope this book reflects the passion you bring to your classrooms, programs, and communities. Thank you for being an inspiring part of this journey.

GERALDINE "GIGI" WYNN

Thank you to my heavenly Father, who is my guiding light.

I want to thank my incredible husband, Antoine, for always supporting me. You are my other half. Thank you for staying up late nights to hear my thoughts, give me ideas, and bring me joy during this process. You inspire me to reach for the moon, and it is appreciated. Thank you to my daughter, Noelle, for your love and encouragement and my boys (Julian, Doanavan, and Joshua) for believing in me. I love you all so much.

To my InspiHER Squad for believing in me and encouraging me to do the impossible, I love you and thank you. To my friends who have never doubted me and provided the right words of encouragement at the right time, thank you.

To Teresa, thank you for seeing "me" and letting me soar. It is an honor working with you. Thank you to Cathy and Sarah for always being supportive, encouraging me, and creating a place of belonging. To my University of Nevada, Reno Extension team (past and present), you hold a special place in my heart. Thank you for your love, encouragement, and support.

To early childhood educators and leaders everywhere, thank you for your hard work and dedication. Thank you for providing little hearts and little minds with a space to grow and develop. You are always essential and one of a kind.

DANIELLE PERTILE

I would like to thank Brandon for his unwavering support throughout the writing process, listening to my endless ideas and tangents and always being ready for the next adventure. Thank you to Artie, who brings joy and light to every day. To my wild and wonderful family, both blood-related and chosen, and to Book Club, I am so thankful for your support and enthusiasm. And to Lu, huggysquigglebuggykissy.

To Monica Salazar, Stephanie May, and Cindy James, thank you for always Spiraling Up with me and helping our experimental little program soar to new heights. To Geri Devereaux, Cathy Peshlakai, and Teresa Byington, thank you for showing me what it means to be a truly great leader and for challenging me to grow into my own leadership.

To the early childhood education community of Nevada: From Reno to Elko, Ely to Las Vegas, and every place in between, you are making an incredible difference in the lives of children and families.

This book belongs to all of you. You have my endless gratitude.

CHARMIKA "MIKA" HANSEN

I am deeply grateful to my children, Tahoe and Sierra, who are my constant source of inspiration, joy, and purpose. Your laughter, curiosity, and resilience remind me every day why the work of uplifting others matters so deeply. To my mother, Linda, whose unwavering love, support, and encouragement have carried me through life's challenges. Thank you for always believing in me, even when I doubted myself. To my siblings, Yasmin and Kinney, I wouldn't be who I am without you both. You get me and you know me better than anyone ever will. I'd also like to acknowledge my late father, who above all, always valued education and would be so proud to see his daughter become an author.

To my incredible team at University of Nevada, Reno Extension, my former colleagues, and the many teachers and leaders I have had the privilege to learn from and work alongside: Thank you for your dedication, wisdom, and heart for this field. To

Teresa, thank you for seeing potential in me that I never recognized in myself. You have given me the push that I didn't know I needed. To Gigi and Danielle, I couldn't have asked for more intelligent, creative, and ambitious women to take this writing journey with.

I also want to acknowledge every single person who works tirelessly, often without the recognition they deserve, to nurture and educate young children. Your passion shapes futures, transforms communities, and keeps the spirit of early childhood education alive. This book is for you.

Introduction

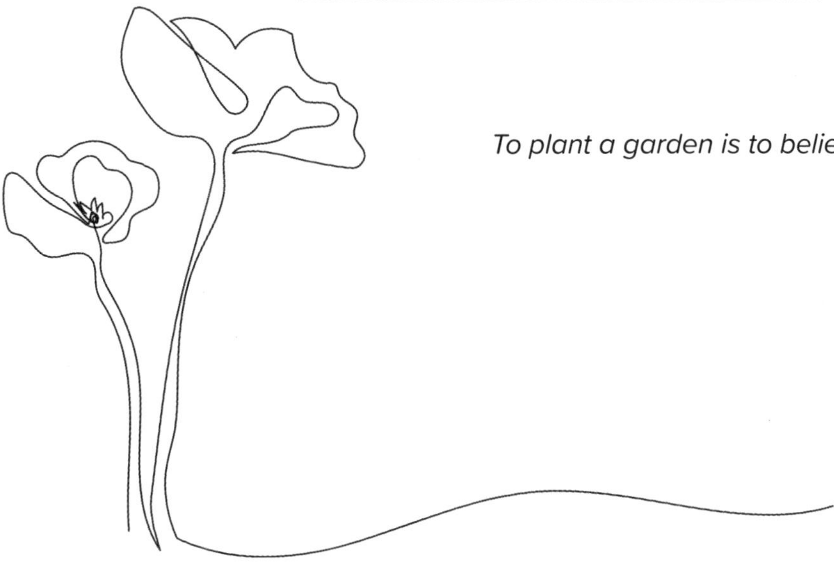

To plant a garden is to believe in tomorrow.

—Audrey Hepburn

Step into the garden, where joy takes root and leadership blooms. Walk down the garden path and discover how uplifting yourself and others can transform the soil of early childhood education. Uplift is the sunshine we offer one another as we lead with our hearts and elevate others with grace, joy, and purpose. Uplift is the intentional act of cultivating positivity, encouragement, and growth in ourselves and others. We uplift others when we choose kindness over criticism, build genuine connections, and express gratitude. As the gardener, you nurture hope, foster connections, and believe that growth is possible, even in challenging seasons. You may need to pull out some weeds of negativity to help joy take root. You may need to replant some seeds to improve the harvest. The important thing is not to give up. Continue to thoughtfully grow your garden, and the world will be a better place.

Throughout this book, we will be interweaving themes of gardening and growth. These themes will be tied to ideas associated with being an uplifting and joyful leader. You will find practices, stories, and reflections that will help you cultivate a culture of joy. You are invited to slip on your gardening gloves, take a breath, and get ready to begin planting something beautiful.

FIVE ESSENTIAL TOOLS

Gardeners use a variety of tools to care for their plants and, similarly, effective leaders benefit from having specific tools to cultivate and guide their teams. Let's explore five essential gardening tools and how they are related to leadership practices.

The first essential gardening tool is a shovel, which is used to prepare and loosen the soil when planting seeds. Likewise, effective, and uplifting leaders prepare the "soil" by digging in and laying the foundation for a strong and uplifting workplace. Leaders also dig into challenges and uncover solutions. They cultivate meaningful relationships and engage team members in creating a shared vision and purpose. An example of a shared vision is "to create a joyful and uplifting environment where everyone has the opportunity to thrive."

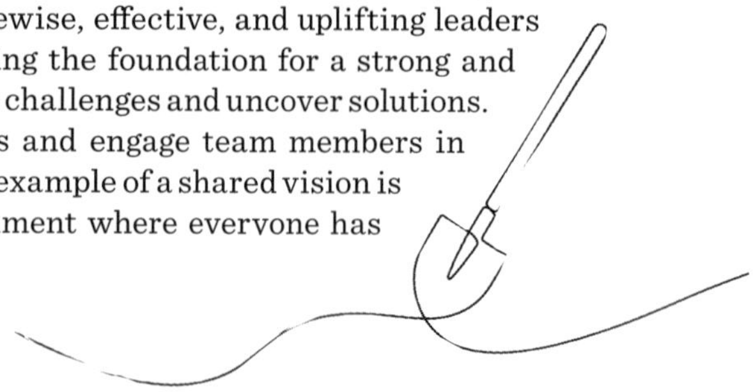

The second essential gardening tool ing can. Watering plants regularly is necessary for their optimal growth. Effective and uplifting leaders consistently "water" their team with appreciation and encouragement. They nurture and support individuals as they grow and develop, fostering a positive work environment designed to elevate morale and motivate team members to collaborate and be creative. Individuals are more likely to thrive when their efforts are recognized, and sincere appreciation is given in a timely and consistent manner. One early childhood leader allocated 30 minutes each morning to visit classrooms and share genuine and specific feedback with teachers either verbally or by leaving a written note. This practice resulted in her team members having increased motivation and engagement. They felt connected and valued.

The third essential gardening tool is a trowel, a narrow hand shovel designed for detailed work like moving small amounts of dirt or meticulously weeding plants. Its sharp, pointed tip offers precision and control. Likewise, effective and uplifting leaders are intentional about paying attention to details and focusing on individual needs. They are mindful and considerate as they interact with members of their team. They take time and engage in intentional actions to learn more about the concerns and challenges individuals may be experiencing and to provide support and resources when appropriate.

Gardening gloves are the fourth essential gardening tool. They give the wearer protection from thorns and rough soil. Effective and uplifting leaders help their team

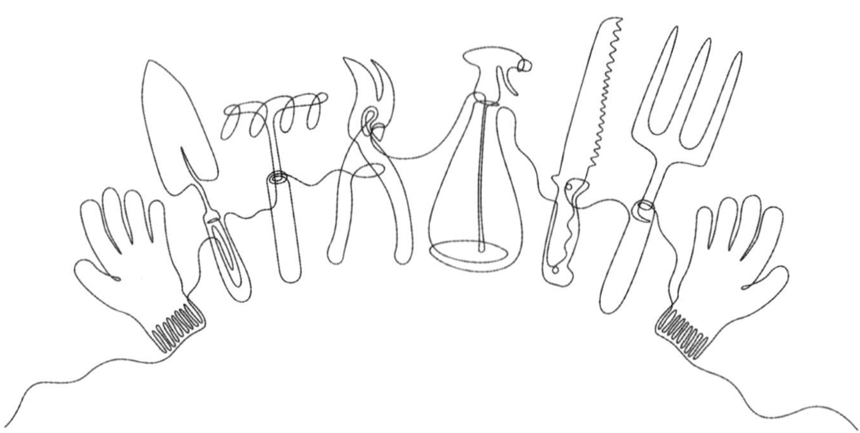

members feel protected and supported. They strive to safeguard the well-being of each person by acting as a buffer that protects team members from unnecessary stress. This provides their team members with more time and energy to focus on the children and their families.

The fifth essential gardening tool is pruning shears, which are used to trim, shape, and remove dead and overgrown branches. Plants that are properly pruned become healthier and more vibrant. Effective and uplifting leaders make tough but necessary decisions. They address challenges, set boundaries, and make changes that will help their team become stronger. These leaders help their team grow as they strive to create strong and vibrant communities. By utilizing these five tools, effective leaders can guide and cultivate their team into a joyful community.

NAVIGATING THIS BOOK: YOUR INVITATION TO PAUSE AND REFLECT

Within each chapter, you will be invited to "pause and reflect" as you consider how you would approach a situation or implement a new strategy. At the end of each chapter, you will find a list of ideas on how you can practice "uplift in action." Additionally, we have included several questions for individual reflection and questions that could be discussed with a group of leaders such as a book group that meets regularly to discuss chapters in the book.

It is through small and simple things that we can have a powerful impact on others. You are invited to pause and reflect as you think about essential leadership tools.

PAUSE AND REFLECT

- What are the essential leadership tools that strengthen your leadership?
- What additional tools could you add to your leadership toolbox? Write down some ideas.

ELEMENTS FOR OPTIMUM GROWTH

Just as a garden requires specific elements for optimum growth, teams also need the right conditions to flourish. Seeds grow best in nutrient-rich soil, with sufficient water and sunshine. A skilled gardener understands that plants have varying growth cycles, adapting their care with the correct amount of water and nutrients.

Likewise, specific elements are needed for the optimum growth and development of teams. A team's nutrient-rich "soil" is an environment that includes trust and meaningful relationships. These relationships are strengthened when team members receive regular watering or words of appreciation and encouragement. Team members thrive when they receive warm rays of positivity and leaders highlight their talents and strengths.

Leaders recognize that their team members have a variety of experiences and diverse perspectives. Each person is growing and developing at different rates and timetables. Effective and uplifting leaders seek to nurture each person's diverse strengths and abilities while also challenging the individual to stretch and expand their skills and capabilities.

PAUSE AND REFLECT

- What elements do you and your team need for optimum growth?
- How can you stretch and expand the skills and capabilities of the individuals that you lead?

Iris and The Children's Garden

Throughout this book, we will be sharing stories about Iris, a new director at The Children's Garden, a childcare center that is struggling with a myriad of issues. You will learn about the challenges and opportunities that Iris faces at work and at home. The stories will illustrate the strategies that Iris uses as she strives to create a joyful and uplifting environment. Iris's story is a composite of the stories of several directors that we have had the privilege to work with over the years.

Iris's story will primarily take place at The Children's Garden, a fictional childcare center consisting of four classrooms: an infant, a toddler, a preschool, and a pre-K classroom. There are two teachers in each classroom, and the administration team includes an assistant director and an administrative assistant.

THE JOYFUL UPLIFT DIFFERENCE

The authors of this book have over 90 combined years of experience in the early childhood field. We have been infant, toddler, and preschool educators, childcare center directors and assistant directors, coaches, and trainers. We are very aware of the struggles and joys of being in the field of early childhood education. We hope this book will inspire leaders and teachers to be part of a movement focused on joyfully uplifting others. We refer to this as the "Joyful Uplift Difference." We have seen the difference that this movement has made in our lives and the lives of the individuals we lead, coach, and train.

To illustrate the profound impact of this philosophy, we'd like to share some stories that embody the Joyful Uplift Difference.

Teresa A. Byington

Lead author of Chapters 1, 6, and 10.

As I watched the TEDTalk "Where Joy Hides and How to Find It" by Ingrid Fetell Lee, I realized that joy was an ingredient that was often missing in my leadership. I resolved to become a joyful leader and find more joy from within. This decision changed my life and the lives of the individuals that I lead. As my team and I focused on being more joyful and uplifting others, our relationships deepened and our creativity was amplified. There was more laughter and fun in the workplace. Our productivity increased, and we were given new and exciting opportunities to share with others how to be more joyful and uplift others.

I received a note from one of my team members that exemplifies how a joyful and uplifting workplace culture can make a powerful difference in the lives of others. She shared that she didn't realize how "unjoyful" she was until she changed jobs and came to work for my team. She was inspired by the way we talked and presented ourselves. She realized she needed to change and be a better version of herself by finding joy from within and spreading joy to others. These actions changed her life and work in a positive and uplifting way. This is just one example of how my team has been impacted by the Joyful Uplift Difference.

Geraldine "Gigi" Wynn

Lead author of Chapters 4 and 9.

The concept of "joy" and how to experience it was introduced to our team in 2020. Although I have felt joy occasionally, this new lens on how to experience joy was different. I have always had a heart to inspire and uplift the individuals around me, and I never dreamed about how it would change my life. Taking the time to explore having joy with my team, family, and friends sparked a feeling in me that this was a choice. I needed to decide how I would show up for myself every day at every moment of my life. I found myself "chasing joy" daily.

Within this work it is easy to become overwhelmed, stressed, and burned out. I genuinely believe we can intentionally want to uplift others if we first understand the importance of uplifting ourselves. My hope and desire are that as you read the chapters in this book, you will discover how to uplift yourself and inspire others to be their best self.

Danielle Pertile

Lead author of Chapters 2 and 5 and coauthor of Chapter 8

In my role coordinating the Spiral Up Academy, I train and coach early childhood educators, most of whom are in their first three months on the job and often are navigating the survival stage of teaching (Katz, 1972). Over three years of coaching, I've learned that while strategies for behavior support, engaging play, and family partnerships are important, what new teachers need most is to feel uplifted. A warm greeting, a listening ear, and genuine recognition of what they're doing well can transform their confidence and competence in the classroom.

This belief comes from my own journey. I've worked in environments shaped by both uplifting and discouraging leadership. In one center, a leadership shift brought a focus on money, productivity, and appearances rather than people. Morale plummeted, joy disappeared, and many, including me, left. Later, I joined my current team, where leaders intentionally nurture joy and uplift their staff. The change was like sunshine breaking through clouds; I knew my worth, not just because of my output but because my contributions were acknowledged and celebrated.

This Joyful Uplift Difference directly impacts morale, retention, and job satisfaction. I've seen the contrast: Teachers supported by uplifting leaders approach coaching with curiosity, hope, and resilience, even during challenges, while those under punitive leadership often feel discouraged and disengaged. I chose to coauthor this book because I want all early childhood educators to thrive, and I believe that when leaders embrace the Joyful Uplift Difference, they build the confident, competent workforce that children and families deserve.

Charmika "Mika" Hansen

Lead author of Chapters 3 and 7 and coauthor of Chapter 8

For as long as I can remember, optimism has been my compass. As a child who moved often, I learned to embrace each new adventure with curiosity and an open heart. A positive mindset helped me build connections, turn strangers into friends, and make unfamiliar places feel like home.

That spirit of joyful uplift has guided my professional journey. When I moved to Buffalo, New York, to become a lead infant teacher, I joined a classroom with two co-teachers who were understandably hesitant about a new lead. Rather than charging ahead, I chose a gentler path—leading with kindness, respect, and a focus on the good. I celebrated their strengths, collaborated on decisions, and built trust through genuine connection. Over time, we grew into a true partnership rooted in communication and shared joy.

This approach extended beyond the classroom, enriching my relationships with staff, teachers, and management. I found deep friendships and a sense of belonging that made my California heart feel at home in snowy upstate New York.

Today, in my role at University of Nevada, Reno Extension, I'm surrounded by a phenomenal team that shares this mindset. Together, we lead with positivity, compassion, and kindness in service to the early childhood education community. I believe that when we approach others with optimism and a spirit of partnership, we create joyful spaces where everyone can thrive. That, to me, is the heart of the Joyful Uplift Difference.

COME WALK THE GARDEN PATH

You are invited to walk down the garden path and discover new ways to joyfully uplift yourself and others. As you meander down the path, we will share how you can tend to your own well-being with kindness and intention; uplift others through your words, actions; and presence and lead with joy, even when the path is uneven. With each turn, you'll uncover ways to care for yourself, nurture others, and cultivate a culture where joy can grow, even in the most unexpected corners.

Just as gardens flourish with sunlight, water, and care, so does a joyful learning environment. The pages in this book contain a variety of seeds, tools, and bites of nourishment to help you grow into the uplifting leader you are meant to be. Let's walk together down this garden path of joy, encouragement, and renewal and discover how powerful it is to joyfully uplift ourselves and others.

As you travel down the garden path, we will explore Iris's story of growth as an early childhood leader. In Chapter 1 you will learn ways to grow strong roots and branches of joy as you nurture and care for yourself and others. Chapter 2 focuses on the importance of uplifting ourselves first, and Chapter 3 outlines five ways to uplift others in the workplace. Ideas for uplifting others by building connections are shared in Chapter 4, followed by strategies for creating an uplifting workplace in Chapter 5. You will learn about the power of playfulness in Chapter 6 and how to implement the HEART framework for addressing challenges within the workplace in Chapter 7. Strategies for joyfully uplifting families can be found in Chapter 8, and we will explore how to manage change with confidence in Chapter 9. Then, in Chapter 10, you are invited to continue to enhance your practices as a joyful uplifting leader and embrace "uplift in action" as you create your own joyful uplift leadership legacy. As you journey down the garden path, take time to pause and reflect on the ideas shared. Just like a gardener studies the soil before planting, your own self-awareness is the foundation for growth. Think about what brings you joy and when you have felt uplifted. What do you do to uplift others? During your quiet contemplation, you will begin to see the roots of your leadership and the blossoms of your impact. Reflect on how you can become a more joyful and uplifting leader.

What will you do to make a Joyful Uplift Difference?

1

Roots and Branches of Joy

Teresa Byington

When I was a young child, my teacher gave me a paper cup, and I was instructed to fill the cup half full of soil and then plant a tiny sunflower seed. I watered the seed and then waited very impatiently for it to grow. Each day as I arrived at school, I would eagerly go look at my cup, but I only saw dirt. Then one day, when I had almost given up hope, I saw a green sprout coming up through the soil. I was so excited and frequently checked on my plant to see how it was growing.

One day, my teacher told our class that it was time to take our plants home because they were getting too big for our little cups. Our flowers needed to be planted outside so they could continue to grow and flourish in the warm sun. I took my little plant home and found the perfect location for it in my backyard. I dug a hole and carefully placed my precious seedling into the ground. I watered it and then I just sat and watched it for a long time. Perhaps I was hoping I would see it grow and bloom right before my eyes. It didn't, but I was still filled with wonder. It seemed impossible that my little seed would one day become a beautiful flower.

Days turned into weeks, and my seedling grew taller, sprouting green leaves, and eventually a bud. Then the day arrived. My sunflower bloomed. With excitement I ran inside to share the news with my mother, and she came outside with me. We laughed and did a happy little dance. We felt joyfully uplifted.

Uplifting ourselves and others begins by planting the seed of joy within yourself. A seed has the potential to become so much more. Likewise, we have daily opportunities to make a positive difference in the lives of others. Just as a seed grows strong roots when favorable conditions such as water and light are present, leaders grow strong roots as they nurture and care for themselves.

THE ROOTS OF JOY

When seeds are planted in the warm soil, they begin to germinate and grow a little sprout. The roots grow downward, deep into the soil, and the sprout begins to push its way upward toward the sunlight. Leaders can also reach upward toward the light as they dig deep and grow strong roots of compassion, encouragement, and joy.

As the tree sprout becomes a seedling, its stem starts to harden and change color. A thin protective bark encases the stem as the small tree continues to grow. Likewise, the roots of joy flourish as leaders mindfully care for themselves and create a protective bark of self-compassion and love.

The roots of a tree provide a solid foundation, anchorage, and support. However, sometimes their importance can be overlooked, as tree roots are hidden from sight. Tree roots play an essential role as they absorb the nutrients from the soil and transfer them to the trunk, branches, and leaves of the tree. When the roots of a tree are deep and strong, they help to prevent the tree from toppling in the wind. Likewise, leaders benefit from developing strong roots. If leaders overlook their own roots and neglect their personal care, this can have a negative impact on themselves and the individuals they lead, risking the stability of their leadership, much like a tree with shallow roots in a strong wind. To cultivate these essential roots, leaders can focus on three key areas that we will explore in this chapter: deepening your purpose, nourishing your physical and mental well-being, and building strong support networks.

Iris's Story

Iris has been an early childhood director for 15 years. About a month ago, she was asked to move to a different childcare center. It was hard to leave the children, families, and teachers she had grown to love, but she was looking forward to a new challenge. Now serving as the director of The Children's Garden, Iris was surprised by the many issues she encountered upon arrival. Despite her experience, she hadn't expected the level of negativity and resentment among the staff. She found herself working long hours to try to turn things around, but

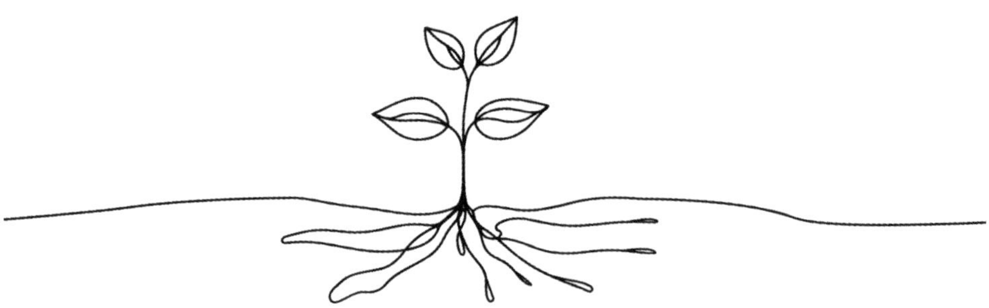

the effort was taking a toll on her. The staff seemed distant and disconnected, and chronic understaffing, combined with frequent callouts, added to the pressure. Iris was feeling emotionally overwhelmed and physically drained. She struggled to sleep at night, her stress levels were high, and recently, she had even snapped at a teacher, something she deeply regrets. She knew things needed to change, but right now, she was simply trying to make it through each day.

PAUSE AND REFLECT

- Can you relate to Iris?
- Have you ever felt burned out, and all you could do was just get through the day?
- What would you do if you were Iris? Write down some ideas.

We will come back to Iris and her situation after we explore some ideas about how to grow strong roots.

GROWING STRONG ROOTS

Within early childhood education, leaders like Iris have many opportunities to make a positive difference in the lives of children and families. Early childhood educators play a significant role in helping children reach their full potential by providing enriching early learning experiences. Children thrive when they have caregivers (parents, teachers, and other adults) that are kind and responsive to their social and emotional needs. Teachers with better coping strategies are more likely to exhibit positive reactions to children's negative emotions (Buettner et al., 2016).

Children benefit from being with early childhood educators who are optimistic and have a cheerful outlook. Interacting with caring adults within joyful and uplifting environments is essential to young children's social-emotional and cognitive development. When we experience positive emotions, it enhances our perspective, encourages curiosity, and improves our ability to solve problems. As described in Barbara L. Fredrickson's broaden-and-build theory (2004), positive emotions can broaden our emotional well-being and build our resilience reservoir. Experiencing positive emotions creates an upward spiral that improves our emotional well-being, leads to greater creativity, and helps us recover more quickly when faced with challenging experiences. Our positive emotions help us grow roots and branches of joy, which play a vital role in uplifting ourselves and others.

Let's explore practical ways to cultivate strong roots in three fundamental areas:

1. Deepening your purpose
    - This involves understanding your "why" and how it connects to your daily actions.

- Create a personal purpose statement and display it as a visual reminder.
- Reflect on past joyful and impactful experiences. When did you feel most fulfilled?
- Engage in a future self-visualization. What kind of leader will you be 5 or 10 years from now? What impact have you made? What joy have you experienced?

2. Nourishing your physical and mental well-being
   - You nourish your roots by eating healthy food, being physically active, and getting adequate sleep. When we feel better physically, we feel better mentally. Nourishing your body can fortify you in fulfilling your purpose.
   - Make time for self-care by doing things that help you feel joyful and uplifted, such as going on a walk or watching the sun rise. You could even combine the two activities and go on a joyful walk as the sun rises.
   - Treat yourself with the same love and respect you want others to treat you with. Tell yourself the same words you would say to a friend if they were in your situation.
   - Listen to uplifting music to improve your mood and decrease any anxiety you may be feeling. Upbeat music increases our brain's production of chemicals such as dopamine and serotonin, our feel-good hormones, which elevate our mood.
3. Building strong support networks
   - Build a strong network of support as you deepen your purpose and nourish your physical and mental well-being.
   - Engage in meaningful conversations. These types of conversations can strengthen relationships and build your resilience. Positive interactions can provide leaders with social support and friendship.
   - Nurture existing relationships. Regularly check in with your network of support.
   - Expand your network strategically. Reflect on the kind of support you need. Seek out mentorship from individuals whose experience and wisdom you admire. Be clear about what you hope to learn.
   - Cultivate diverse sources of support that include friends, family, professional peers, mentors, support groups, and community groups.

Iris called her best friend, Jada, and they talked about some of Iris's struggles. Iris shared that she wanted to focus on creating a positive and uplifting environment, but being short-staffed at work was making her job more difficult.

Teachers were frequently calling out sick, and this resulted in Iris being in the classrooms more often, which resulted in her needing to stay late to complete her administrative tasks. When Iris arrived home, she was exhausted and did not want to do much of anything. Jada asked Iris, "What are several things that you enjoy doing?" Iris shared, "I really liked going for walks, listening to music, and working in my garden, but I haven't taken time to do any of these things recently." Jada said, "I have an idea. Let's meet after work, a couple of times a week, and go on a walk. We could listen to some of your favorite songs or just talk." Iris loved the idea. Having a plan to get together with Jada helped Iris leave work on time. Because she was feeling better, she was completing her tasks more quickly and efficiently. Iris looked forward to being with Jada and was excited to share several songs from her playlist. Walking in the fresh air invigorated her, and she felt less stressed and ready to face the next day.

Making minor changes can make a difference in how we feel and act. When we have something to look forward to, we feel uplifted. When we can share what we enjoy with others, things become more enjoyable. Joy can be found in small moments, also known as micro-moments.

MICRO-MOMENTS OF JOY

Joy has been described as momentarily experiencing positive emotions that can make us smile and laugh. Ingrid Fetell Lee, in her book *Joyful: The Surprising Power of Ordinary Things to Create Extraordinary Happiness* (Lee, 2018a), emphasizes that joy is distinct from happiness. Joy is usually short-lived, immediate, and often sparked by sensory experiences. Joy can be found in small (micro) and simple things. When you take a few moments to be joyful, it can have a significant effect on how you feel. An example of a micro-moment

of joy is noticing something joyful, such as a young child's smile, and then savoring the joy you feel in that moment.

You can intentionally engage in micro-moments of joy throughout the day by noticing joyful things within your environment. You can even create micro-moments of joy through your words and actions. These simple acts could have an influence on how you feel and act.

PAUSE AND REFLECT

- What could you say or do that would be joyful?
- How can you create a micro-moment of joy? Could you share a fun photo or tell an amusing story?

Finding and recognizing joy can change how we see the world. The Greater Good Science Center at the University of California–Berkeley in collaboration with other research institutions has been studying the impact of engaging in "micro-acts" of joy by inviting people to participate in the BIG JOY Project. Over 117,000 participants from more than 220 countries have been part of the BIG JOY Project (see https://ggia.berkeley.edu/bigjoy).

Participants in the BIG JOY Project are invited to engage in one micro-act of joy each day for a week. These micro-acts of joy include sharing a laugh, doing something kind, or celebrating another person's joy. Preliminary results from the study indicate that participants who engaged in micro-acts of joy during a one-week period experienced a 25% increase in their emotional well-being and had increased feelings of hope and optimism. Let's explore several ways you could add micro-acts of joy to your work as a leader.

Add Joyful Laughter

When we laugh or hear others laugh, we often feel more joyful. If you need a quick pick-me-up, watch a short video of children laughing or another funny video. You will find yourself laughing because laughter is contagious! Laughter can elevate your mood and help you feel better.

Experience the Awe of Nature

Have you ever been in a forest or on a mountain top and looked around and experienced a moment of awe and wonder? Our natural world is full of beautiful sights. When we tune into the natural world, we can experience a sense of awe as we feel the power of the waterfall and the majesty of the trees in the forest. It is energizing. Being in nature can also be healing and help us feel calmer and more balanced. One leader shared that watching a short 2-minute nature video was like taking a mini-vacation. She felt awe as she saw scenes of waterfalls, hummingbirds, and whales jumping in the ocean. Even better than a video is spending time outdoors by going for a walk or driving to a park and experiencing a sense of awe and wonder.

As Iris continued to go on her walks with Jada, she noticed more things in her environment. She saw a bird singing in the tree and the pink flowers blooming in the field. She felt the gentle breeze on her face and heard the bubbling brook. She breathed deeply to take in the smell of freshly cut grass and could almost taste the orange blossoms. Her senses felt renewed.

Make a Gratitude List

Take a moment and reflect upon the goodness in the world. Think about things that bring you support, comfort, or opportunity and create a gratitude list. When we are grateful, we recover from stressful and upsetting events quicker and have more meaningful relationships with others. Focusing on things for which you are grateful can also lead to more optimism about life, increase physical comfort, and produce better health.

Noticing and writing down what you feel grateful for can bring goodness to mind and help relieve any tension or stress you may be feeling. Our brains tend to focus on what is wrong instead of what is right. You can train your brain to focus on the good by sharing what you are grateful for with others. This act can enrich your relationships. Take a few moments to feel grateful for the good things you have in your life.

After several months of going on walks together, Iris wanted to express her gratitude to Jada for being such a valuable friend. She wrote Jada a heartfelt letter sharing her appreciation for the times they had spent together laughing and crying. She told her how spending time together had made such a significant difference in how she felt, and it had pulled her up when she was feeling down. She thanked Jada for her listening ear and for the miles they had spent walking together.

Take a Mindful Joy Break

Take a mindful break by pausing. Close your eyes and take three mindful breaths. You engage in mindful breathing by focusing your attention on your breath and noticing how your breath is coming in and going out. As you take each mindful breath, reflect on how you are feeling at that moment. Relax your mind and body. Think about something or someone that brings you joy. Continue to breathe in and out. Savor the moment and then open your eyes. Think about how you are feeling. Did you enjoy your mindful break?

As we become more mindful of our emotions, thoughts, and feelings, we gain a greater understanding of ourselves and our well-being. By focusing on joy, we become more aware of joyful things.

Do a Kind Act

Kindness is being considerate and generous. It is often seen as individuals engage in thoughtful actions. Kindness is showing someone else you care.

When we do kind things, it gives our brains a boost, and that feels good. Being kind can help take our minds off our worries. We are kind when we give people the benefit of doubt instead of judging them. Kindness includes giving a compassionate response, helping someone complete a task, celebrating milestones, and acknowledging personal achievements. You can spread kindness by bringing in a surprise treat to brighten someone's day or giving your undivided attention during conversations and respecting personal boundaries. When we are kind, the recipient and the people that witness the kind act are more likely to be kind in the future because kindness is contagious.

Give Yourself a Shout-Out

Take a moment and give yourself a shout-out. Remind yourself of all the things that you have accomplished. Reflect on how you have positively touched the lives of children, families, and coworkers. Think about your purpose and why you became part of the early childhood community. What you do matters. Acknowledge and appreciate the positive difference you are making in the world by nurturing and educating young children and their families.

Celebrate the Small Stuff

Celebrate the small stuff by having a joyful micro-celebration. Find a party hat or noise maker and celebrate the person who arrives at work early or is willing to stay late. Create a traveling badge or crown and involve your team in recognizing anyone that goes above and beyond. Take time to celebrate and create a micro-moment of joy. Why wait for the big events to celebrate when you can find something to celebrate every single day?

Iris felt refreshed. Going on walks with Jada had lightened her load and given her something to look forward to each week. They had fun together and laughed often. Jada was always encouraging Iris to try something new. One of Jada's ideas was for Iris to give out smiley stickers to everyone she saw smiling at her childcare center. Iris decided to see how many smiling people she could find on Friday. She purchased a large roll of smiley stickers and went to the front door. As each person arrived, she smiled at them and gave them a sticker and wished them well. She was amazed at how many people smiled when she smiled first. She gave out lots of smiles and stickers!

PAUSE AND REFLECT

- What micro-acts of joy can you add to your work as a leader?
- How could you add more joyful laughter or a sense of awe and wonder to your day?

BRANCHES OF JOY

As a tree establishes strong roots, branches form and reach upward and outward, away from the trunk of the tree. Just as branches of a tree grow upward and outward, leaders can spread joy by reaching out, uplifting, and creating joyful experiences for the individuals they lead.

When the tree branches become strong, they provide structural support for the leaves, fruits, and flowers produced by the tree. The branches become the conduit that carries the water from the soil to the leaves. Likewise, when strong leaders support the individuals they lead, they give them strength and encouragement to grow and develop.

Tree branches grow upward reaching toward the light. Leaders can be a light by uplifting the individuals that they lead. Leaders can help their team reach higher heights and flourish by supporting each person in their individual journey.

We asked leaders to share what they do to uplift others. Here are some of their responses.

- Recognize and acknowledge the unique strengths that each person brings to the team during meetings or one-on-one conversations.
- Start your day by smiling and maintaining a positive, encouraging tone even during challenging moments.
- Give authentic responses and practice active listening: Pause, reflect on what you hear, and validate feelings before responding.
- Lighten the mood. Share a funny moment or be playfully silly when the time is right.
- Create a safe, judgment-free space by listening with openness and without interruptions or judgement.
- Tell your team how their work is making a difference in children's and family's lives. Be specific. Remind them of their impact and the contributions they are making.
- Respond to tough situations with empathy and compassion; highlight what is going well alongside opportunities for growth.
- Offer clear opportunities for their personal growth and professional development, such as training, mentoring, and leadership roles.
- Do daily check-ins, even brief ones, to show you're available and present when someone needs support.
- Show concern during challenging times; assemble a thoughtful care package when someone's health (mental or physical) is affected or someone has lost a loved one.

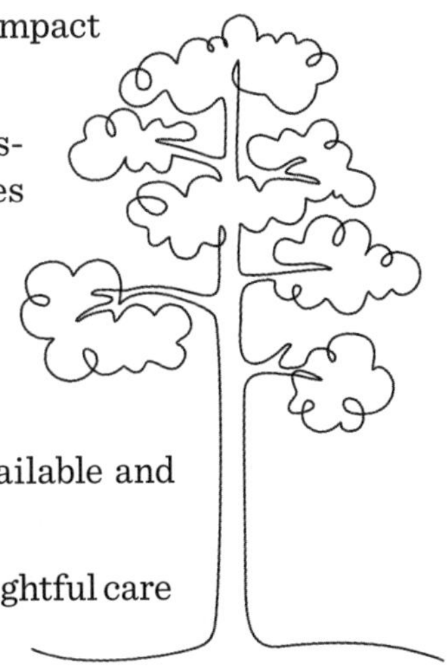

- Invite a team member out for coffee and a genuine conversation, no agenda, just time to make connections.
- Say "thank you" often and express gratitude in personalized, meaningful ways. Hearing you express what you are thankful for about them is impactful.

PAUSE AND REFLECT

- What do you currently do to uplift the individuals you lead?
- What else could you do? Write down some ideas.

Iris's Approach

Iris was finding more ways to bring joy into the lives of the children, families, and teachers that came to her center. She started each day by greeting the children and families with a big smile. When she went into a classroom, she focused on the good things she saw and took time to share something positive with the teachers. Iris added a big bowl of positive quotes to her office that teachers could stop by and read whenever they needed a little lift. She became more intentional in thanking her team for their efforts, especially on hard days. Iris also had fun doing the unexpected. One day she came to work wearing a big fancy hat and passed out homemade treats to everyone. She also involved her team, and together they planned special days such as Pajama Day and Favorite Book Day, where everyone was invited to bring in a favorite storybook.

An interesting thing happened. As Iris's team became more engaged and joyful in their work, fewer staff were calling out sick. Her team was having more fun, and their enthusiasm had trickled down to the children and families. There was a greater sense of playfulness and joy at her center, and Iris looked forward to coming to work each day.

You do not need to do it alone. Collaborate with your team to create a culture that prioritizes joy and uplifting others. Deep and lasting change happens when we are engaged in daily actions that make a positive difference. As we uplift others, we will feel better, and in turn, so will the people we interact with throughout the day. Celebrating small wins along the way helps maintain momentum. If everyone strove to joyfully uplift themselves and others, the world would be a better place.

Mark Williamson, the director of Action for Happiness, an organization focused on helping people create a happier and kinder world, shared that you can act your way into a new way of thinking and feeling much more easily than you can think your way into a new way of acting. When you take time to act, your actions will change your thoughts. If you wake up one morning and do not want to get up and go to work, you can think about getting up all day, but until you act and get up, not much is going to happen. It is important to act; get up and meet your day with positivity and joy.

PAUSE AND REFLECT

- What actions might you take to create a better world?
- How can you meet your day with positiveness and joy?

Here are some examples of action that early childhood leaders across the United States are taking to bring joy into the lives of early childhood professionals.

Health and Wellness Day

One leader shared that her leadership team was concerned about the mental well-being of their employees, and they received permission from their administration to initiate a Health and Wellness Day once a year. During the Health and Wellness Day, early childhood educators can select activities that they want to participate in from a menu of choices. Choices include going on a hike, painting pottery, going out to brunch, or sharing ideas in a book club. The entire morning focuses on each person's emotional health. In the afternoon, everyone comes together to hear from a speaker whose message is focused on positivity and joy. Teachers have shared that the day fills their emotional buckets and helps them feel happier, healthier, and ready to begin a new school year.

Mad Hatter Tea Party

Another organization, the Kansas Child Care Training Opportunities, has an annual Mad Hatter Tea Party Training Day. It has been held on the first weekend in March since 2014. The event venue is decorated with white rabbits, teapots, and mad hatter–style hats. Participants receive training on topics that include literacy, storytelling, science, and music. Learning is interactive and fun. During breaks, participants enjoy petit fours, specialized cookies, teas, and other beverages. One of the highlights of the event is the Hat Contest. Everyone is encouraged to decorate and wear a festive hat. Prizes are given for the most creative hats: the Mad Hat, the Madder Hat, and the Maddest Hat. It is a joyful event.

Recognizing the Helpers: Thank You Luncheons

One organization holds an annual luncheon for all the maintenance and warehouse staff that work for their company. The leadership team pays special tribute to the contribution the employees make in keeping their facilities clean and well-run. This annual event uplifts individuals that are often unrecognized for their efforts.

Turning Tasks Into a Party

Have you ever asked your team to do something and it did not get done? One leader, who oversees early childhood educators at multiple locations, had asked her staff to laminate the materials from a new curriculum. She discovered that many of them had not done the task, and she was concerned about the durability of materials, so she organized a laminating party. She set up times at each of the locations and arrived with the laminating machine, snacks, and music. Everyone had fun and all the laminating was completed. Staff told her they were looking forward to the next "work" party.

Setting Up a Recognition Board

Another way to uplift others is by creating a recognition board. This is a board where individuals can thank others for something they have done. Team members are encouraged to write a fun note about something they noticed, to express gratitude, or to celebrate successes and place it on the board.

One organization selected a different theme for each month of their recognition board. In February, everyone was invited to write what they "love" about their coworkers on a paper heart. In November, they had the opportunity to write down something they were thankful for on a colorful fall leaf.

There are many opportunities to be involved in uplifting and joyful actions. Remember that both the roots and the branches of joy play important roles in your growth as an effective and uplifting leader. Uplift yourself and then uplift others.

SUNFLOWER ANALOGY

Leaders bloom as they discovered their roots and branches of joy. The reawakening can be likened to this sunflower analogy. Sunflowers are bright and cheery yellow flowers that people often find joyful. The yellow petals of a sunflower shine and glimmer in the sunshine. Likewise, leaders that are bright and cheery will be seen as being joyful.

Let's continue to compare sunflowers to leaders. Sunflowers have deep roots. These roots grow slowly so they can support the sunflower as they grow tall and strong. Likewise, leaders need to take time to grow deep roots so they can be strong and resilient when challenges arise.

Sunflowers receive nutrients and nourishment from the soil that are absorbed by the roots and transferred up the stem to the leaves and flower. Leaders can nourish their roots with nutrients that will help them feel physically and emotionally healthy.

As the sun rises each morning, young sunflowers turn toward the sun's light. The sunflower follows the sun as it rises in the east and sets in the west.

At night, the sunflower closes, and rests for the night. Similarly, leaders can follow the light by looking for the positive in each day and taking time to rest and recharge at night.

Sunflower branches and leaves are lifted toward the sky. Once sunflowers are fully nourished, they attract bees and insects seeking pollen. Leaders are more successful at giving nourishment to others after they have first nourished themselves. When leaders share joyful "pollen," people will come to them seeking the light and positivity they have to share.

THE JOYFUL UPLIFT DIFFERENCE

We can each seek to become happier and more joyful versions of ourselves. Most leaders want to flourish and be engaged in meaningful work. As you joyfully uplift others, you can create a culture where you and your team can thrive. You will inspire others to strengthen and grow their own roots and branches of joy.

INDIVIDUAL REFLECTION

1. Reflect on how you could grow stronger roots of compassion, encouragement, and joy. What would you need to do?
2. Recall a time when you felt joyful. What was happening? What made the moment joyful? Determine several ways you can intentionally engage in micro-moments of joy every day.
3. Think about a time when you felt positive emotions and were uplifted. What are some ways you can create an upward spiral of positive emotions for yourself and others?

BOOK GROUP OR DISCUSSION QUESTIONS

1. What are some actions leaders can take to become more joyful versions of themselves? How can you extend your branches of joy to others?
2. What types of work are meaningful to you as a leader? What are meaningful actions that leaders can take to joyfully uplift others within the early childhood field?
3. What actions can you take as a leader to create a more joyful and uplifting atmosphere at work? Is there an uplifting event that you could initiate with the individuals you lead? Share your ideas.

UPLIFT IN ACTION

Select one or more of the following to practice uplift in action.

- Immerse yourself in an awe-inspiring moment.

- Write down at least seven things in your life that you are grateful for, such as the air that you breathe or loving family and friends.
- Express gratitude to at least one person that has made a difference in your life sometime this month.
- Do a kind act.
- Plan and then have a joyful micro-celebration.

2

Uplifting Ourselves First

Danielle Pertile

ROOTS OF JOY: THE ACACIA TREE

When moving into our new home in 2015, my husband and I were so happy to see the beautiful desert landscape that had been planted in the front yard. The yard included an acacia tree, which is well adapted to desert living. I imagined the future of our front yard: the tree strung with holiday lights or dotted with ghosts and spiders during Halloween time. I could picture myself washing my car in the driveway under its shade (and shade is a luxury in the hot Las Vegas sun). The tree continued to grow and provide its greenery and shade for a few years, but one year we experienced an extreme windstorm, with winds reaching 50–60 miles per hour. The next morning, my family was devastated to see that the acacia tree had fallen over. We called a tree service to come out and remove the tree. Once finished with the cleanup, the service person told us that the tree's roots just weren't deep or strong enough to support the size of the tree in that kind of a storm.

If the roots of joy mentioned in Chapter 1 provide us with the nourishment, strength, and encouragement to continue through the storms of life, what happens when those roots are weak or shallow? My acacia tree looked healthy and strong on the outside; it did its job of providing shade on hot days and branches for holiday lights, but all it took was one good gust of wind, and the tree fell. A leader's roots of nourishment, joy, and renewal must be strong enough to weather the gusts that threaten to topple them. As a leader, are you ready for the next windstorm? In what ways do you strengthen and uplift yourself amid the challenges you face?

In this chapter, you're invited to reflect on how you nourish your roots and explore practical ways to embody the three concepts of self-compassion, self-care, and self-uplift. As we discuss what it means to care for and uplift ourselves, it's important to acknowledge the many challenges leaders face in putting these practices into action, especially the common feelings of guilt or hesitation when making time for personal well-being. We'll also explore realistic, manageable strategies for weaving small, meaningful moments of self-care and self-uplift into your daily leadership practices. It must be acknowledged that the topic of self-care is deeply nuanced; culture, gender, socioeconomic status, age, and many other factors influence how we view self-care. I encourage you to examine your feelings as you read through this and to implement the strategies that feel good to you and help you feel uplifted.

SELF-COMPASSION, SELF-CARE, AND SELF-UPLIFT

In the early childhood field, leaders are often focused on their "branches and leaves," which includes their outreach, the children and families they serve, the people they lead, and their impact on the community. These are important and worthwhile concerns, but leaders must also continue to nourish their roots by creating a strong foundation of self-compassion, self-care, and self-uplift. By nourishing the roots, leaders protect themselves from the everyday storms and become more effective and joyful leaders. Self-care, self-compassion, and self-uplift are three distinct practices that can work together to build resilience, strengthen your mind and body, and bring lasting joy into your life.

Self-Compassion—Tilling the Soil

Self-compassion is a new term gaining attention in the field of psychology. While self-care focuses on the mind and body, and self-uplift focuses on creating joyful overflow, self-compassion is the practice of being kind to yourself. Kristin Neff, who coined the term, explains that self-compassion is an internal reflective practice that takes place throughout the day (Neff, 2011; Neff et al. 2020). This practice is like tilling the soil in a garden; you are creating a habitable environment for wonderful things to grow.

An important component of self-compassion is self-kindness. How often are you intentionally kind to yourself? When did you say something kind to yourself, forgive yourself for making a mistake, or even pay yourself a little compliment? Being kind and compassionate to ourselves is much harder than projecting that same kindness and compassion outward to others.

In the leadership community of practice of which I am a member, I asked early childhood leaders what challenges they face in uplifting themselves. Many of their answers sounded something like

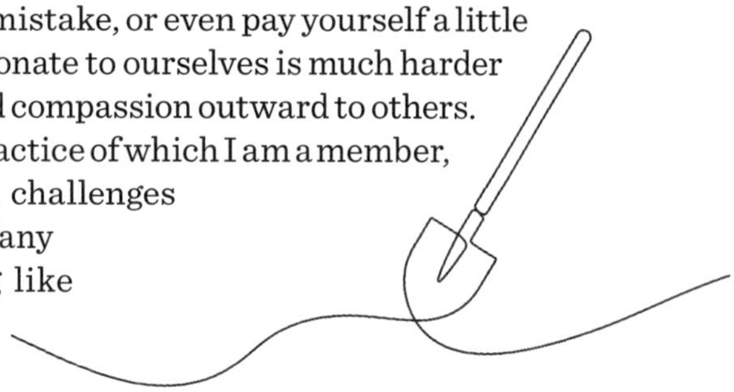

this: "I dismiss my own accomplishments as 'just doing my job.'" "I often don't consider myself, and when I do, I am my own biggest critic." "[I often have] negative thoughts and self-doubt." And "I'm so hard on myself." Does this feel familiar? If so, know that you are not alone.

Leadership can sometimes be a thankless job, and it's easy for the negative messages we receive to turn inward and become our own self-talk. Self-compassion is the practice of disrupting that negative self-talk with something positive. Imagine that you are pulling the weeds of your garden as you till the soil, the weeds will only choke out the beauty. A simple way to practice this reframing is to ask yourself, "What would I say if my best friend said this about themselves?" As you become aware of your own negative self-talk, respond as you would to your best friend: "You are capable." "You've got this!" "You are amazing!" Practicing this positive self-talk is a mindful behavior that has been linked to stronger mental health and shown to increase self-compassion (Grzybowski & Brinthaupt, 2022).

Self-Care—Pruning the Branches

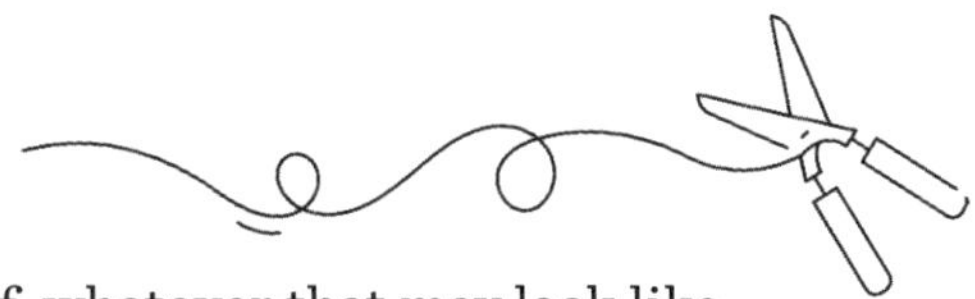

Self-care is the simple act of caring for yourself, whatever that may look like. Some people practice self-care by taking a long, hot shower. Others practice self-care by eating a nutritious meal or spending an evening playing a favorite video game or watching a TV show. Prioritizing your health by going to regular doctor and dentist check-ups can be considered self-care. The practice of self-care looks different for everyone; what works for some may not work for others. It's important to acknowledge that some of the suggestions throughout this chapter may not work for you, and that's OK. Self-care begins with simple choices you make during everyday routines to prioritize your own mental, emotional, and physical health. Self-care is like pruning a garden; capable gardeners will cut certain branches and leave others to support healthy growth. It may be uncomfortable at first, but the plant soon thrives and ends up producing more flowers or fruits than it would have without the pruning.

Unfortunately, the term "self-care" has become so tangled in meaning that it often feels unattainable or unrealistic. The "wellness industry" (or "wellness influencers" or "wellness bloggers," etc.) might have us believing that to truly practice self-care, you must have regular spa days, buy $16 smoothies, take expensive yoga classes, and "treat yourself" to material possessions. Social media feeds are often filled with photos of luxury vacations, pricy handbags, and freshly smoothed wrinkles, all tagged with "#selfcare." These things are great if they work for you, but it's important to remember that the wellness industry is in the business of making money, not supporting your well-being. True self-care is often achieved through small acts that, when practiced consistently over time, build into routines that support our long-term health and well-being (Kanold & Boogren, 2022).

Self-care and self-compassion go hand in hand. Self-compassion helps us recognize our needs and respond to them with kindness, while self-care is the action we take to meet those needs. For example, self-compassion might sound like *"I didn't meet that deadline. It's okay to feel upset,* and *I can still treat myself with kindness in this moment."* Self-care might follow with *"I'll give myself more time for the next assignment,"* or *"I'll say no to new commitments while I focus on this project."* In this way, self-compassion creates the foundation for self-care, and self-care, in turn, creates the foundation for self-uplift.

Self-Uplift—Blooming

"Self-uplift" is a term developed for this book to encapsulate the idea of not only compassionately caring for yourself but also having fun and seeking joy while doing it. Think about an activity or a hobby that brings you joy. It might be reading a good book, baking something delicious, practicing art or music, being out in nature, cuddling with pets, or something else entirely. These simple pleasures are often the first things to be pushed aside to make room for more work, chores, accomplishments, or commitments, but these things deserve your time too. Self-uplift is the culmination of your self-compassion and self-care practices, where the groundwork has been laid for healthy roots and the branches have been carefully maintained. Now, it's time for the flowers to bloom and feel the warmth of the sun.

A popular phrase in the education field is "You can't pour from an empty cup." This is true in theory, but in practice, educators and leaders are too often filling their cup just enough to pour their last drops into others. Alternately, some of us will start and stop self-care practices, unsure of what our bodies and minds need to feel refreshed. This is like pouring from a cup with a hole in it; we may be trying to pour into ourselves, but it does not sustain us. What the phrase "You cannot pour from an empty cup" means is that what you pour into others should be your *overflow,* not your last dregs. Self-uplift is the practice of filling your own cup to the point of overflow. From that overflow you can, in turn, pour into others and nourish them without depleting yourself. See Table 2.1 for descriptions and practices.

PAUSE AND REFLECT

- How will you care for yourself this week?
- What is one kind or uplifting thing you can say to yourself right now?
- What activities or hobbies bring you joy?

Iris's Story

Iris had been with The Children's Garden for 6 weeks, and was struggling to find her footing and balance in her work as director. The staff struggled to work collaboratively and to implement the center's curriculum and daily routines, and because of that, the children often presented challenging behaviors in the classrooms. This had been going on long before Iris started, and parents were

Table 2.1. Filling Your Own Cup

Name	Description	Practices
Self-compassion *Tilling the soil*	Being kind to yourself, treating yourself with compassion, and positive self-talk Becoming aware of your needs	• Pay yourself a compliment • Notice what you've done right • Talk to yourself as you would to your best friend
Self-care *Pruning the branches*	Taking care of your physical, mental, and emotional health Meeting your needs	• Eat meals that nourish your body • Practice good sleeping habits • Take breaks • Set boundaries around your time, attention, and energy
Self-uplift *Blooming*	Seeking joy and making time for your passions Exceeding your needs so you can then pour into others	• Identify activities or practices that bring you joy • Spend intentional time on your passions or hobbies • Share your passions and hobbies with others • Focus on your "why"

beginning to notice and complain. Iris felt that she didn't have a moment of peace when she was at work; there was always a fire to put out.

At home, Iris faced additional challenges. Her teenage son often had difficulty focusing at school, and she frequently received calls from the school informing her that he had been reprimanded for his behavior or was falling behind in his work. While Iris's husband was supportive, he often worked long hours and went out of town for his work, so many of the daily struggles would fall, again, on Iris's shoulders.

Iris often found herself feeling alone and overwhelmed. She knew she needed to take care of herself as well as her family and her staff, but with so many demands on her time and attention, self-care was often the first thing to be put aside so she could deal with all the minor emergencies at hand.

PAUSE AND REFLECT

- What advice would you give Iris about how to find time to take care of herself and manage her stress?
- How can Iris uplift herself?

UPLIFTING OURSELVES AMID CHALLENGES

We know now that the combined practices of self-care, self-compassion, and self-uplift work together to fill our cup, but what happens when we get down to those last dregs of what we can give? Too often, those of us in professional caregiving fields find ourselves spending so much time and energy uplifting and caring for those around us that we neglect caring for and uplifting ourselves. This is a surefire way to burn out. "Burnout" has become a common phrase in the early childhood education field over the last few years due to rising demands of the job, tight licensing and accreditation guidelines, stagnated pay, limited funding, and many other factors. Research suggests that burnout is one of the leading causes of early childhood educators leaving the field (Fox et al., 2025; Schaack et al., 2020). Burnout is a state of physical, emotional, and mental exhaustion after feeling the effects of stress for too long and is the result of pouring from an empty cup too often; the cup is not only empty, but dry.

In caregiving fields such as education and health care, another specific term may apply when stress is chronic and becomes more than burnout: compassion fatigue. Compassion fatigue is the intense physical and mental health exhaustion caregivers experience when exposed to constant stress or trauma by caring for others. Can it really be a bad thing to *care too much*? It turns out that caring for others without balancing care for yourself can lead to negative consequences for your physical and mental health as well as putting your career at risk (Erdman et al., 2020).

According to the Compassion Fatigue Awareness Project (2017), symptoms of compassion fatigue may include bottled up emotions, preoccupation, mental and physical tiredness, chronic physical ailments such as gastrointestinal problems, nightmares, compulsive behaviors, apathy and sadness, substance abuse, and legal problems. All of this can stem from putting others before ourselves. This might be compounded if you are also a parent or a caregiver at home as well as in the workplace.

It's also important to recognize the impact that trauma has on early childhood educators. The focus of so much research has been on the impact of trauma on young children, but we must also acknowledge that early childhood leaders and educators may be coming into their work having experienced their own trauma. As a leader, becoming trauma-informed is so important to support your staff in responsive and individualized ways (Jeffrey et al., 2022). It's also important to help you understand and work through trauma you may have experienced. When working with our own or others' trauma, patience and gentleness are key. You can be gentle and patient with yourself as well.

Earlier in this chapter, Iris recognized the importance of self-care, but the reality is that she was the lowest of her own priorities. In caregiving fields, there is a level of guilt associated with self-care. We are care*givers*, not care*takers*. This was compounded in 2020 when the COVID-19 pandemic rocked the world and made the term "essential personnel" an everyday household phrase. Across the country, childcare workers still showed up to work every day even though many other businesses were shut down and thousands of people were working from home, because they were essential to a functioning society in the United States. That's a lot of responsibility on the shoulders of educators! During that time, educators fled the profession in the thousands. The industry still has not rebounded, which puts even further strain on those that remain (Goldstein, 2022). How do we combat burnout and compassion fatigue? Prioritizing self-compassion, self-care, and self-uplift are good starting points, as these practices can support your mental, physical, and emotional health in the long term.

GIVING OURSELVES PERMISSION

Every human being is born with the capacity for joy, and like the pilot light on your stove, it still burns within you even if you haven't switched on the burners for a while.

—Ingrid Fetell Lee (2018a, p. 10)

When was the last time you turned on the burners of your own joy? Do you ever feel like you're not allowed to, especially when others need your attention? In our work with early childhood leaders, the theme of permission often arises when discussing self-care and self-uplift. Many professionals feel they're not allowed to prioritize themselves—that doing so is selfish, radical, or even shameful. There's a fear of letting others down, causing inconvenience, or taking energy away from those they serve. I've heard from many educators and leaders who carry guilt around meeting their own needs. Have you ever felt that way? You're not alone. But here's the truth: When we neglect our own wellness for too long, we eventually run on empty with nothing left to give. And that helps no one, least of all ourselves.

Before we can go any further in discussing uplifting ourselves, there must be permission given for these practices. Not from your boss or those you lead, or from your partner or children, and not from society, but from yourself. What if you gave yourself permission to take that hour and go to the gym? What if you gave yourself permission to close your office door for 30 minutes to eat your lunch in peace? What if you gave yourself permission to take an annual leave day to lie on the couch and watch your favorite guilty pleasure show? What if you gave yourself permission to breathe deeply for 30 seconds and focus on that breath and nothing else?

What might it look like if you grant yourself permission to care for and uplift yourself? You are encouraged to do this in a tangible way, even if it feels uncomfortable at first. Say out loud, "I don't have to earn self-uplift or self-care," or "I'm going to take care of my needs first today." You may also write down an action plan for self-uplift for the day, the week, or the month. Another option is to develop a mantra and repeat it to yourself in your head. Many educators and leaders with whom we work find difficulty in just acknowledging their own worthiness when it comes to being uplifted and practicing self-care. If you can acknowledge that you deserve care and uplift and give yourself permission to care for yourself, that is the first step toward uplifting yourself.

Cultural context plays a significant role in how educators perceive self-care and self-uplift. Some may feel greater pressure to appear strong, suppress stress, or "keep a stiff upper lip," depending on cultural expectations (Villalobos et al., 2024). A self-care practice that feels empowering in one culture may not resonate in another. That's why it's essential to reflect on your own cultural lens when considering what self-care and self-uplift can look like for you and what practices truly feel meaningful.

Now that you have given yourself permission, let's turn our attention to what self-care and self-uplift may look like for you.

SMALL BITES OF SELF-CARE

A lot of information has been written about self-care practices. You may already be familiar with practices such as mindful breathing practices, positive self-talk and practicing affirmations, or using movement and exercise as a way to improve your physical and mental health (Balban et al., 2023; Mu et al., 2024). What becomes difficult is finding or making time for these practices when your schedule is already packed to the brim most of the time, and adding a new practice to an already full schedule is often easier said than done. The thought of "one more thing to do" can feel overwhelming, leading us to set it aside entirely. Each time we delay caring for ourselves, it becomes easier to say, "I'll get to it tomorrow," or "maybe next month." Eventually, we forget all about it and fall into the same patterns that bring us to the brink of burnout.

When approaching self-care, it's important to be realistic and take small steps until you find something comfortable, meaningful, and sustainable (Kanold & Boogren, 2022). Early in my leadership journey, I received valuable advice: plan for "small bites" of self-care. I rarely have time to take a luxurious bubble bath or go for a solo hike, but I can care for myself in smaller increments of time. In ten minutes, I can practice a few stretches at my desk. In five minutes, I can eat a healthy snack. In one minute, I can breathe and practice mindfulness. These small moments throughout the day can be just as meaningful as longer, more intentional rest periods.

PAUSE AND REFLECT: *How will you practice small bites of self-care?*

- In one minute, I can take care of myself by:

  ____

- In five minutes, I can:

  ____

- In ten minutes, I can:

  ____

FINDING AND SUSTAINING JOY: SELF-UPLIFT PRACTICES

A focus on our own joy and well-being is anything but selfish.
It is the most positive thing we can do for the world.

—Nancy Rosenow (2023, p. 94)

Now that we have given ourselves permission to care for and uplift ourselves and have identified ways to practice small bites of self-care, it's time to consider how we can uplift ourselves daily by creating opportunities for joy. Below are a few ideas to help you build a lifelong practice of self-uplift.

1. Remember Your "Why"

Have you ever sat down and intentionally thought about or written down your purpose in the early childhood profession? Why do you do the work you do? Defining and remembering your "why" can help you find clarity within your work; it can steer you toward your long-term goals and help you avoid side-tracks or pitfalls (Byington, 2023). It's necessary to discover and live in your "why," because that is what will sustain you in the long run when things get difficult (and we *know* they'll get difficult).

PAUSE AND REFLECT

- What drew you to this field?
- What aspects of your job bring you joy?
- When do you feel like you are your best self, professionally?

Joy Journaling and Uplift Sprinkles

Both joy journaling and uplift sprinkles are practices that you as a leader can implement as a way of keeping a running record of good things. These similar but unique practices allow you to compile uplifting, meaningful, and joyful moments from your work and can support you during challenging seasons.

Joy Journaling. In my coaching sessions with new early childhood educators, I ask them at the beginning of all our discussions, "What brought you joy in your work this week?" At first, they don't always know how to answer. Their answers are usually simple joys such as "A child was excited to see me when I came in on Monday," or "I got a hug this morning." As our sessions continue, they begin to expect the question and share deeper "joy moments." I start to hear answers like "I was really struggling with a child's behavior recently, but I made an effort to connect with him this week and that made a huge difference!" When we intentionally look for these joyful aspects of our work, we begin to see them everywhere, and we see them in sharper focus. These moments can help you more fully understand and live within your "why," or purpose, as an educator and a leader.

As a leader, I encourage you to look for and write down one small (or large) thing that uplifts you in your work every day, or even once a week, either as they occur to you or at a scheduled time. This is the practice of joy journaling. Perhaps you made a connection with a new parent who was previously skeptical about child care, or it could be that you were able to get your monthly budget completed on time! These may not always stand out as typical joyful events, but aren't they still uplifting? These small things can build the foundations of self-uplift that sustain us in our work. Over time, you will accumulate pages of positive memories to revisit when you need a morale boost or just want to remember why you do this work. These moments can help you connect more deeply with your purpose as a leader.

Uplift Sprinkles. Whereas joy journaling helps you collect meaningful aspects of your work over time, uplift sprinkles provide a lighthearted way to collect sweet memories and anecdotes. I have a running notes document on my phone in which I write down any funny thing my son says. Some of my favorites are "How do we have pictures of dinosaurs? Because cameras weren't invented yet, and humans weren't invented yet!" and "That was the magicest thing I ever saw." I have been writing down his observations and one-liners practically since he started speaking, and I still read through them and laugh out loud at his insights. I'm thankful I started this practice when he was so young, partly because it is like a time capsule of his thoughts throughout the years, but also because it brings me joy to reread his silliness when I need a moment of joy. These are my uplift sprinkles.

You might implement uplift sprinkles by using a jar or basket with slips of paper, or like mine, a running document with small but uplifting insights that can be collected over time. You can write down funny, meaningful, or special moments that happen in your work and slip them in with the other uplift sprinkles to read again later. You may have a communal uplift sprinkles collection in your staff lounge, in which staff add funny moments with the children or "caught you being awesome" moments with their coworkers. As with your joy journaling, you can revisit these insights whenever you need a morale boost or even just a laugh.

PAUSE AND REFLECT

- What brought you joy in your work this week?
- What felt like a win for you this month?

2. Sharing Your Joy With Others

Earlier in this chapter I described self-uplift as engaging in practices that bring you joy. Many joyful hobbies and practices are ones that can be shared with others. For example, I love to bake and will often bring fresh batches of chocolate chip cookies into the office to share. When I share something I've made, it brings me even more joy than just the act of baking itself.

What hobbies or self-uplifting practices do you have that you could share with others? If you like to create art or music, how can you share that with the children and staff in your center? If you enjoy cooking or baking, bring a little extra to put in the staff room at lunchtime. If you practice yoga or meditation, lead sessions in the classrooms with children. Sharing with others what makes you feel joyful can bring you even more joy. A note about this: If sharing your joy ultimately feels more like work than joy, *don't share it.*

3. Dress for Joy

My favorite musical of all time is the 1969 classic *Hello, Dolly!* with Barbra Streisand. One of the biggest musical numbers in the film is where the whole cast sings about getting dressed up in their finest to make a big trip to New York City. They sing about how you can't feel sad when you wear your "Sunday clothes," or the attire that makes you feel put together and joyful. I think they were onto something there; have you ever slipped into your favorite dress, pair of sneakers, or jeans that fit you *just right* and had the brief sparkly feeling of joy? The sparkly feeling might just give you a little more bounce in your step as you walk through the doors of your workplace as well.

Back in the 1980s, women entered the workplace with their "power suits": shoulder pads, heels, and big hair. This was a way of women communicating their power and readiness to get to work. Power suits may not be the hot trend anymore (though I have seen shoulder pads making a comeback), but choosing clothing or accessories that bring us joy can boost our confidence in the workplace. Research shows a direct link between what we wear and how confident we feel at work (Adam & Galinsky, 2012; Horton et al., 2023). It's remarkable that something as simple as clothing can positively impact our confidence on the job.

What would "dressing for joy" look like for you? Is there something in your closet that gives you that sparkly, confident feeling? For me, it's red lipstick. I wear it almost every day because it makes me feel bold, powerful, and joyful. My coauthors each have their own joyful style: Teresa loves wearing purple or blue with matching accessories. Gigi has an amazing collection of colorful sneakers and sometimes rocks a pair of shiny or vibrant heels. Mika often brightens our office with bold-patterned dresses. Dressing for joy isn't about impressing others with a power suit; it's about choosing clothing, accessories, or shoes that boost your confidence and add a bounce to your step.

Iris's Approach

Iris spent time reflecting on her work duties and the obligations in her life outside work. She knew that the level of pressure she was under was not sustainable for her long-term mental, physical, and emotional health. While there are no quick fixes, Iris began to put a few new strategies into practice to make her overall wellness her top priority. She first gave herself permission to care for herself by writing down her plan on a sticky note and sticking it to her computer monitor. Seeing it each morning when she entered her office helped Iris feel more connected and committed to her goals. Iris scheduled time in her daily task calendar to take a 10-minute stretch and breathing break twice a day. Each afternoon before she left, Iris wrote in her notebook one positive thing that happened that day and one thing about which she was proud. In the staff room, she implemented an uplift sprinkles basket filled with the funny things children said in the classrooms that week, which brought joy to herself and her staff.

A few weeks later, Iris noticed she was beginning to prioritize self-care at home too. She kept up her walks with her friend Jada and started spending more time in her garden, where her mind could rest and her hands stayed busy. She invited her son to join her, creating meaningful time together as they prepared for the week ahead. When her garden yielded a bumper crop of tomatoes and peppers, she brought baskets of fresh produce to share with staff and families at the center.

THE JOYFUL UPLIFT DIFFERENCE

Uplifting yourself isn't a luxury to squeeze in at the end of a busy day, and it doesn't require spa days or expensive gym memberships. The truth is that extra time rarely appears, and self-care isn't always in the budget. The drive to uplift yourself must come from within. It starts with recognizing that you are worthy of care. Give yourself permission to prioritize your well-being, and look for small moments throughout the day to do so. It might be as simple as taking a few deep breaths or going for a short walk during lunch. Or it might mean creating a deeper practice, like joy journaling or aligning your schedule with your "why." When you uplift yourself first, you're better equipped to uplift others without burning out or experiencing compassion fatigue. You are absolutely worth the care you give yourself.

INDIVIDUAL REFLECTION

1. How did it feel to consider prioritizing your own needs and joy before others'?
    a. What would you tell your best friend about prioritizing their needs and filling their own cup?
2. Reflect on ways you can create and share joy in your workplace.
3. Create an action plan of what, when, and how you plan to care for yourself this week.

BOOK GROUP OR DISCUSSION QUESTIONS

1. How can leaders practice self-uplift? What would this look like in your organization?
2. What are ways leaders can share the concepts of self-care, self-compassion, and self-uplift with the teaching staff? What would it look like if those concepts were encouraged for all staff?
3. What other strategies have you found in the past that bring you joy, rest, or peace?

UPLIFT IN ACTION

Select one or more actions to uplift yourself today.

- Take three deep box breaths.
- Write down or say out loud "I give myself permission to uplift myself."
- Write down one aspect of your work that brings you joy.

3

Uplifting Others in the Workplace

Charmika "Mika" Hansen

Years ago, at the beginning of my career, I taught preschool at a center led by a director who had a small but powerful habit: Every morning she would walk into the center, visit each classroom with a warm smile, and say something uplifting. "I love how you set up your classroom today, Ms. Lopez!" Or "Ms. Daniels, you handled that tricky situation with such patience yesterday. I really admire that."

At first, it just seemed nice, and I didn't think much of it. But over time, after I had experienced several other workplaces, I realized that director's positivity was uncommon and quite contagious. The teachers at that center complimented each other more, shared more moments of encouragement, and found ways to lift each other up more than in any other program I had worked for. The energy was greater, brighter, and happier. Even on tough days, there was always a sense of support and camaraderie that made all the difference.

Having the pleasure of working with this director taught me such a valuable lesson: Uplifting others doesn't require big, dramatic changes. It's the little things, the words we say, the kindness we extend, the moments of connection we create, that transform a workplace into a place of joy.

THE APPLE TREE

Within the intricate landscape of our professional lives in early childhood education, there exists a powerful and often overlooked force that bears the fruits of compassion, inspiration, and joy. Imagine the concept of uplifting others as a magnificent apple tree with the magic to transform our workplace relationships and experiences. Join me on a walk through the orchard as we explore how what we pour into those around us can be the seeds for our own growth. In a world that often emphasizes individual success, the power of uplifting others is the choice that will make all the difference.

In Chapter 1, we explored the importance of strong roots—how a leader's foundation supports the entire team. Then, in Chapter 2, we focused on uplifting ourselves, recognizing that when we nurture our own well-being, we have more to give to those around us. Now, we turn our attention to the heart of our work: uplifting others in the workplace. Think of your daily interactions as nourishment—small but meaningful actions that enrich the soil of your workplace culture, allowing the roots of a united team to grow strong and deep. With this in mind, let's approach each day like a picnic! Picture your team joyfully gathered under the refreshing shade of our uplifting apple tree. Think of every kind gesture, moment of connection, or expression of gratitude as a freshly picked apple shared between colleagues. We have the power to cultivate a ripple effect of positive influence within our own professional worlds. Let's examine the art of changing our own perspectives and discover practical strategies that can help you cultivate an uplifting workplace culture.

MY 2022: HOW UPLIFTING OTHERS HELPED ME HEAL

Uplifting others is a topic that resonates deeply within my own personal life and has extended its positive impact into my professional life, as well. In the ebb and flow of life, it is easy to fall into the mindset of "every man for himself" when we face our fair share of challenges and obstacles. However, the power of lifting others up is a force that has helped me heal and transform my life in more ways than I can measure.

According to the Holmes and Rahe Stress Scale (Holmes & Rahe, 1967), here is a list of the top 10 most stressful events that humans can experience (in no particular order):

1. Death of a loved one
2. Marriage, separation, divorce, or relationship issues
3. Incarceration
4. Starting a new job or losing a job

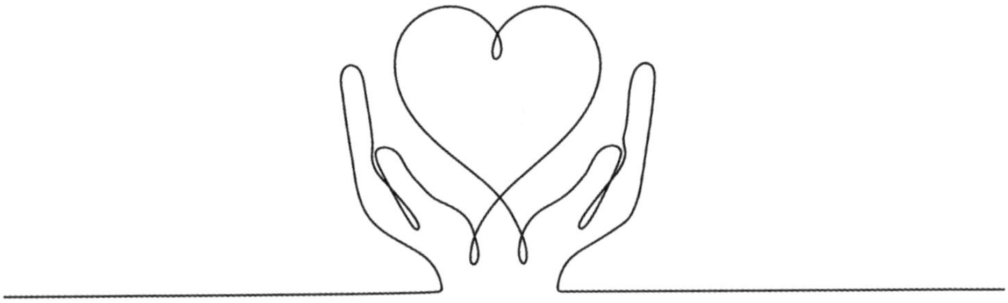

5. Workplace stressors
6. Financial problems
7. Moving, buying, or selling a home
8. Serious illness or injury
9. Having a baby or adding a new family member
10. Retirement

As you read through that list, I am sure you can relate to several stressful life changes; such is the human experience. Let's explore my life in 2022. During that year I mourned the sudden loss of my father to a heart attack (#1), separated from my husband of 7 years and got officially divorced (#2), started a new job as an early childhood education trainer and coach after being a stay-at-home mom for 3 years (#4), was lucky enough to purchase a new home for me, my two children, and my goldendoodle (#7), and officially adopted my daughter (#9). As an honorable mention, I was also diagnosed with anxiety and depression, and my therapist suspected I also had ADHD (she was right). Needless to say, 2022 was the hardest year of my life, yet I was able to find and hold on to so many moments of joy through it all.

Change Your Perspective

Changing my perspective is truly what carried me through the last few years. I prioritized joy, gratitude, and uplifting others. Instead of focusing on the negative and throwing myself a pity party, I focused on others. I poured my heart and soul into my children, working to bring them joy through so many changes. I found ways to support my mom and bring her joy while she mourned the loss of her husband. I leaned on my amazing siblings, and we brought each other moments of joy as we grieved together. I immersed myself in my job as a trainer and coach, doing my best to uplift the wonderful teachers that I work with. I even found myself giving more grace to strangers, as I realized that you never truly know what someone could be going through. When I focused on bringing joy to others, I brought joy to myself! I invite you to take a moment and think of someone you know who is experiencing life challenges. Maybe, after today, you can find a way to bring a little joy into their lives.

PAUSE AND REFLECT

- Have you experienced any of the 10 most stressful life events listed? How did others uplift you? How did you uplift yourself?
- Think of a difficult situation you are currently experiencing. Is it possible to change your perspective?

Tierra's Story: Before Iris

Tierra often thinks about her birthday last year. She was already dreading work when her alarm jolted her awake that morning. Tierra had worked at The Children's Garden for five years and she was unhappy. She prepared for the day hoping that the center wouldn't be understaffed again. As she drove to work, Tierra wondered if she could sneak into the classroom before the director, Beth, noticed her. Every time Beth saw Tierra, she found something regarding the center to complain about. The night before, she made Tierra stay late for the third night in a row without a word of thanks. As Tierra clocked into her morning shift, she braced herself as the director came out of her office looking stressed. "I have a mountain of work and Lori quit today! You're lucky you're only a teacher. That reminds me, I will probably need you to stay late." Tierra nodded, thinking of the dinner plans that she would have to cancel.

Tierra tried to uplift her spirits as she walked down the hall to her classroom. She'd been trying her best to hide the burnout, but she knew the children could tell something was off. Tierra greeted her preschool students, and her co-teacher, Anna. She immediately noticed the sad look on Anna's face. She shared that Beth, the director, shot down her idea for a family art event. Tierra felt horrible because she knew how much courage it took Anna to even ask. Just then an announcement from the assistant director came over the PA system: "Just a reminder that every teacher is responsible for keeping the playground clean after each use. I just came from outside and it was such a mess! You will be written up after your first verbal warning." At this moment, Tierra sighed and thought, "I wonder if anyone will wish me a happy birthday?" No one did.

Have you ever been in a work environment like the one described above? Chances are that we all have experienced a negative workplace in one way or another. Whether you have dreaded walking into the building, been taken advantage of as an employee, or felt completely undervalued as an important part of the team, the effects of a negative workplace can severely impact your overall mental health and quality of life (Fehr et al., 2017). The antidote is uplifting others! When leaders make uplifting others a daily priority, they can completely transform the workplace culture into one that cultivates a sense of pride, joy, and community. Here are five simple strategies that you can start using, right now, to uplift others in your workplace.

FIVE WAYS TO UPLIFT OTHERS IN THE WORKPLACE

1. Start With a Warm Welcome

A surefire way to uplift someone in the workplace is to help them feel valued and welcome from the very beginning. I have had the pleasure of working with my team at the University of Nevada, Reno Extension, for several years. When I arrived at my cubicle on the first day of work, *this* was what was waiting for me. I couldn't believe it! There were several welcome signs, my favorite candy and

snacks, lots of books to set me up for success, and fun things like a journal, a candle, gum, a pinwheel, motivational cards, and more! This type of warm welcome brought me so much joy. I felt lucky to be a part of such a joyful team and eager to do a good job. Throughout my time there, I have seen this happen to newcomers on the team, and you can clearly see what a positive impact it makes on a person.

Our department recently welcomed a wonderful new employee, Stephanie, to our team. Here is how she described her first day: "Of all the jobs I've ever had, I have never felt so valued! From the moment I walked into the office, I was greeted with a smile and told how excited everyone was to have me on the team. My cubicle was decorated with a welcome sign and my desk was covered in fun little gifts. I was speechless and I even teared up a little. I was just so pleasantly surprised. Throughout the day, everyone on the team took time out of their day to say hi and personally welcome me. By the end of the day, I just knew I was in the right place."

As a leader in the workplace, your warm welcome might look completely different. Other warm welcome ideas include having the new employee fill out a "Get to Know You" questionnaire (see Appendix A on the Brookes Download Hub for a reproducible version), treating your new employee to lunch, assigning the new employee an onboarding buddy for the first month, having the children in their classroom create art for the new employee, or having the whole team sign a welcome card. The possibilities are endless. No matter how you approach an employee's first day, I encourage you to include the following every time:

- a smile and expression of how happy you are to have them on the team,
- a welcome gift, card, or personalized note,
- staff introductions and a tour of the workplace, and
- assurance that employees can come to you with any questions or concerns.

These simple things will start your working relationship on a high note!

PAUSE AND REFLECT

- What made you feel welcome on your first day of a job?
- In your current role, how can you add joy to a new employee's first day?

2. Show Sincere Appreciation

Cultivating a community of gratitude in the workplace starts at the top. Find moments to genuinely express appreciation for your team's efforts, acknowledging that their important work directly contributes to the success of the center (Fehr et al., 2017). As a leader, your words carry more weight than you may realize. Never underestimate the impact of a well-timed acknowledgment or an unexpected compliment. Creating consistent moments of feeling seen and valued are the building blocks of a motivated team with a clear sense of purpose. Don't be surprised when you notice those around you start to express feelings of gratitude more often.

Need some ideas? We asked a community of child-care center directors in Las Vegas, Nevada, how they currently uplift their employees. Here are their responses in regard to showing sincere appreciation:

- "I like to encourage them: You got this!"
- "I write down different joyful quotes for my team."
- "I make it a priority to point out things they have done and personalize appreciation to the individual."
- "We have a board where staff can shout out each other for the great things happening every day."
- "I bring in treats!"
- "I simply say thank you all the time."
- "We hand out raffle tickets for longer breaks and extra time off."
- "I love giving my team positive affirmations."
- "We have personalized staff awards at the end of year. Everybody gets one!"
- "We have coffee Fridays!"
- "I like to keep the break room clean and cute and stocked with some sort of snack or drink."
- "I make it a point to remind them of the impact they make on the lives of the children and families we serve."

PAUSE AND REFLECT

- Can you think of a time you felt truly valued within the workplace?
- How can you make your coworkers feel valued?

3. Share Knowledge and Highlight Strengths

Have you ever heard the phrase "What you focus on grows"? It essentially means that where attention is directed often determines what will grow and thrive. Imagine a workplace where each individual is not just recognized for their role but celebrated for their unique strengths. As a leader, your role extends beyond managing tasks and must include shining a light on the strengths that make your team a powerhouse. Show your team that you believe in them by pouring into their ideas and giving them opportunities to shine. Share your own knowledge generously and encourage employees to share with each other, creating an environment where expertise is not hoarded but freely exchanged (Jo & Shin, 2025). When you commit to unlocking potential and empowering your team, you lay the foundation for a culture that thrives on collaboration and mutual support.

A director once told me about a time when she let an employee take the lead on an idea that seemed a little risky. Sharon ran a successful child care center with two infant rooms, two toddler rooms, and four preschool rooms. Scheduling all of the staff every month had always been a nightmare. Between days off and teacher shift preferences, Sharon felt like she was always letting someone down. Finally, Sharon calmly expressed her frustration with the schedule during a staff meeting. To her surprise, Mia, a lead toddler teacher, raised her hand and suggested a solution. "What if you let each age group of classrooms create their own schedules?" This meant that the infant teachers would work together to schedule themselves, the toddler teachers would schedule themselves, and the same for the preschool classrooms. Mia even offered to work with Sharon to create scheduling forms that outlined guidelines for each group of classrooms.

Sharon wasn't 100% sure this idea would work, but she decided to try it out for the next month. Guess what? It was a major success! Sharon found that once teachers were responsible for making sure the schedule worked for the needs of their classrooms, they were more flexible and considerate of each other. To this day, the teaching team for each age group submits their schedules to Sharon every month. Now, her only scheduling responsibility is to review the schedules for coverage and plug in substitutes when needed. Mia had truly solved one of the biggest management problems that Sharon faced for years!

PAUSE AND REFLECT

- What special skills, expertise, or professional talents do you have? Who could you offer to teach or mentor?
- What special skills do you recognize within your team?

4. Show Acceptance and Approval

In early childhood education, leaders can foster a culture of acceptance and approval by embracing diverse perspectives and making sure everyone feels included (Patrick et al., 2024). Flexibility, acknowledging work-life balance, and prioritizing time for teachers will further strengthen a supportive atmosphere. Encourage open and honest communication while demonstrating patience and respect when inevitable conflicts arise. Aspire to be an uplifting leader who is always ready to listen and learn.

Consider this thoughtful Twitter post by organizational psychologist and writer Adam Grant (2022), "It's hard to keep an open mind if you don't have an open heart. You don't have to agree with what people think to learn from how they think. You don't have to share their identity to be curious about what shaped it. Treating people with civility is a prerequisite for discovery." What will you be missing out on if your employees don't feel accepted and comfortable enough to speak up? What problems will go unsolved? What projects will never be started? What successes will be lost?

PAUSE AND REFLECT

- Can you think of a time when you overcame differences with a coworker? What allowed you to find common ground?
- How do you prefer to be approached when someone disagrees with you?

5. Sprinkle Kindness and Celebrate Milestones

Seize the opportunity to spread joy by surprising your colleagues with thoughtful acts of kindness. Consider how it would feel to be gifted a cup of your favorite coffee when you least expect it or to find an encouraging note on your desk when you are having a rough day. Heartwarming gestures like this build connection while often having a domino effect as staff members feel inspired to pay each small act of kindness forward. Make kindness the cornerstone of your daily workplace interactions and you will create an environment of warmth and camaraderie.

In the hustle and bustle of an early education environment, making it a priority to recognize special days can create a sense of delight to break up the monotony. Common milestones to celebrate can include birthdays, holidays, work anniversaries, and employee of the month. Don't forget to use days like National Donut Day or National Red Nose Day as an excuse to have some fun! No matter your budget, simply finding a way to acknowledge these occasions can be meaningful. Stepping in to give someone an extra 15-minute break for their birthday or decorating a teacher's classroom door on her work anniversary are low-cost ways to bring joy to your team. There's always a reason to celebrate, and it's always uplifting to have something to look forward to!

Here are 10 fun ideas for workplace celebrations:

1. Themed potlucks
2. Costume and decoration contests
3. Workplace scavenger hunts
4. Monthly raffles
5. Group arts and crafts projects
6. Themed photo booth with props
7. "Happy hour" delivery cart of afternoon treats
8. Fun personalized awards night
9. Group service projects
10. Game and trivia events

PAUSE AND REFLECT

- Can you challenge yourself to commit one act of kindness in the workplace this week? What will you do?
- What workplace celebration suggestion is the most appealing to you?

Tierra's Story: After Iris

It is 1 year later, and Tierra is still working at The Children's Garden, where Iris was hired as director 6 months ago. As Tierra's alarm goes off in the morning, she wakes up looking forward to seeing her preschool class. It is Space Week, and the kids are having so much fun with the activities. As she gets ready, Tierra makes a mental note to grab a coffee for her co-teacher, Anna, to thank her for transforming the dramatic play area into a fun rocket ship for the kids. On her drive to work, Tierra thinks about sneaking into the director's office to share how much she loved the training on challenging behavior that Iris recommended. She decides to grab a coffee for Iris, as well. After clocking in for her morning shift, Iris finds Tierra first, handing her a card and wishing her a happy birthday. Iris adds that she is impressed with how well Anna is doing in the classroom and thanks Tierra for taking the time to train her on positive redirection. The compliment makes Tierra feel warm inside.

As Tierra approaches her classroom, she notices that the door is decorated with streamers, balloons, and a huge happy-birthday sign. She smiles, and as soon as she opens the door, her students run over, screaming happy birthday and showering her with hugs. She hands Anna her coffee, and Anna hands her a basket of cookies she baked to celebrate. Tierra asks Anna how her meeting with Iris went the night before, and Anna's face lights up. "She loves my idea to have an art event for the families!" Anna shares. "She wants to talk more about how we can make it work within the budget." Just then, an announcement comes over the PA system: "Good morning, all! Join me in wishing our favorite lead Tulips teacher a happy birthday! We are treating you all to afternoon ice cream sundaes to celebrate!" Tierra sighs contentedly, thinking, "I love my job!"

THE JOYFUL UPLIFT DIFFERENCE

Of course, not every day at The Children's Garden was perfect; it was a work in progress. Still, Iris was just getting started, and she knew that meaningful change takes time. Tierra's story shines a powerful light on how genuine, consistent efforts to uplift your team can transform the workplace. Changing one person's day can lead to uplifting a whole community of educators. It starts with one: one person, one small action, or one kind word, or even just one moment of your time. When you start with one, the potential is truly limitless.

Remember that magical apple tree from the beginning of this chapter? The one with the power to transform your workplace? Let's take a little trip back to the orchard. As you lean against the sturdy trunk, consider if this could be another metaphor for the support and encouragement you can foster within your team. Glance up and notice the sunlight shining through the branches, illuminating the contrast between green leaves and bright red apples. Could this represent the beauty of a harmonious community of early childhood professionals? I want to share a secret with you . . . this tree isn't magical at all. It was created with intentionality and consistency. You can grow your own Uplifting Apple Tree in your workplace when you choose to show up for your team every day with joy, gratitude, and an open heart.

INDIVIDUAL REFLECTION

1. How can you change your perspective on a current difficult situation within your workplace?
2. What actions can you take to prioritize uplifting others?
3. How can you show sincere appreciation for the individuals on your team?

BOOK GROUP OR CLASSROOM DISCUSSION

1. What are examples of ways individuals could be warmly welcomed during their first days and weeks of work?
2. How have you given team members opportunities to shine?
3. How could you sprinkle kindness and celebrate milestones in your organization?

UPLIFT IN ACTION

Select one or more of the following to practice uplift in action.

- Greet each colleague you see today with a genuine smile and a warm hello.
- Leave a handwritten note or send a quick message of appreciation to a coworker for something you noticed they did well.
- Invite a team member to share an idea or lead a small project. Celebrate their strengths!
- Bring in a small treat or favorite snack to share in the staff break room as a surprise.
- Acknowledge a workplace milestone (birthday, work anniversary, personal accomplishment) and help organize a simple celebration.
- Offer support or encouragement to a colleague you notice may be having a tough day.
- Start a gratitude chain and encourage each person on your team to “pass on” a compliment or act of kindness to another.

4

Uplifting Others by Building Connections

Geraldine "Gigi" Wynn

Building relationships and creating connections is like cultivating a garden. As much as I love the aesthetics of gardens, I must be honest, I do not have a green thumb. I have had many beautiful experiences receiving flowers and visiting places that are popular and well known for the type of flowers they possess. There are three meaningful memories in my life I would like to share. The first memory is of me as a child playing hide-and-seek at the Rose Garden at Exposition Park in Los Angeles, California. My friends and I would play for hours. It was filled with laughter, joy, and connection. We would run and walk through the garden, pick out our favorite flowers, and share how beautiful the roses smelled.

My second memory is waking up on New Year's Day to watch the Rose Parade with my family. I could not wait to see all the floats covered with beautiful colored roses and the famous people I would see. We would gather on the couch in our pajamas and watch with excitement. I remember my mom cooking in the kitchen to prepare a New Year's Day family dinner and chatting with us about the parade as she cooked.

The third meaningful memory is "Flower Friday." It started when I began dating my husband. Every Friday, for the first two years of our dating, he would buy me flowers. It brought such joy and created a bond between us that is still meaningful today. "You are probably wondering, "Do you still get flowers every Friday after 12 years?" The answer is a beautiful no, but he still brings me flowers on other days of the year. I really need to bring this special tradition back (smiles).

UPLIFTING OTHERS

Uplifting others by building connections as a leader is like harvesting a garden. Sometimes, it requires working together (connections) and valuing each other's differences and perspectives. For example, a rose garden thrives better when planted with garlic, and when beets are planted with onions, it protects the beets from borers and cutworms; this is called companion planting. Companion planting is when fruits, vegetables, and flowers are paired together to help each other grow (Vanheems, 2025).

Uplifting others by building connections is an intentional action that creates meaningful relationships that have the potential to strengthen and nourish your team and the families and children you serve (NAEYC, 2020). Within the three memories I shared, meaningful relationships were at the core. As humans, it is natural for us to crave connection and a sense of belonging. Connection is described as an energy between people when they feel seen, heard, and valued (Brown, 2021).

Iris's Story

The Children's Garden childcare center has a staff of 11 team members to support their children and families. The team ranges from 20 to 50 years of age, and building meaningful connections has been difficult since Iris became their new director 2 months ago. The staff have been frequently calling out sick, and relationships have been strained recently. Shannon and Mei are toddler teachers who work together. During their transition from outside on the playground to lining the children up to return to the classroom, they overheard some team members express how working at this center has been uncomfortable lately due to all the changes implemented by Iris, the director. For example, to ensure that children are safe, they are required to do a name-to-face check and no longer count children. Also, counters in the classroom must remain clutter free. Iris explained how these minor changes will support a safe environment. When they entered the classroom, they both looked at each other with their eyes wide an expression of "OMG!" and began to whisper as they helped their enthusiastic toddlers put their coats away:

Shannon: "Did you hear that?"

Mei: "Yes, they are not happy about the changes Iris has been making. They do not want to do 'name to face.' They think it is ridiculous."

Shannon: "They think the school does not feel the same and they miss how things used to be. They think Iris is trying to control how we clean our rooms."

Mei: "Did you hear them say they are going to keep calling out until they find a new job."

Shannon: "You know, this is going to make our jobs harder, and we will have to do overtime. Ugh! Do you think we should talk to Iris?"

Mei: "Yes. Should we go together?"

Shannon: "Yes."

Mei: "I'm nervous but let's go and talk to her after we close our classroom."

Shannon: "Okay."

Shannon and Mei felt a wave of emotions that consisted of anger, sadness, nervousness, and anxiety during their shift but knew they had to speak with their new director. They both agreed that the school felt different because they missed their previous director, who had a bubbly personality. Iris smiles at times and she is polite but very businesslike. After they closed their classroom, they walked to the front office and asked Iris if she had a moment to talk and listen to a concern.

Iris: "Of course, how can I support you?"

Shannon: "Today we heard a couple of the teachers complaining about how the school does not feel the same."

Mei: "We know you have been working here for only two months and trying to get everything in order, but I have to say that hearing my peers today gave me some anxiety."

Iris: "I am sorry to hear this. Do you feel comfortable telling me exactly what you heard?"

Shannon: "Basically, they are not happy with the changes, and they are going to keep calling out until they find new jobs."

Iris: "Oh my (placing her hand over her chest)! That makes me feel sad."

Shannon: "We are thinking, if they keep calling out, we will have to pick up their slack and do overtime."

Mei: "What are you going to do? I know that this will impact our team, the children, and their families."

Iris: "First, I want to thank you both for being brave enough to come and talk with me about your concerns. This week I will meet with my administrative team and see how we can make better connections with our team about the current changes. Can you give me a couple of weeks, and I will touch base with you on what we are planning to put in place?"

Shannon and Mei agreed to support their new director during this uncomfortable time. Iris immediately set up a meeting with her assistant director and administrative assistant for the following day.

PAUSE AND REFLECT

- Have you experienced staff members not being happy with the changes you implemented within your program? If so, how did they make you feel?
- How do team members' complaints impact your program?

UPLIFT WITH CONNECTIONS

As a leader, balancing what needs to be done in your scope of work versus what the team needs to thrive may be challenging, but it can be done with intention. This chapter will explore three "uplift principles" to help guide you in building authentic relationships that connect you with your peers, children, and families. Ultimately, breaking new ground will create a culture that uplifts people in the workplace daily.

Uplift Principle #1: Encourage Connections

Encouraging connections in the field of early childhood may not be a new concept for you. Whether you are in leadership, teaching children, or participating from a family's perspective, having positive and healthy connections strengthens the relationships around you. The word "encourage" is defined as to inspire and give hope and support with courage (Merriam-Webster Dictionary, n.d.; Oxford Dictionary, n.d.). Encouraging connection requires leaders to possess the skills to model trust, empathy, communication, respect, flexibility, and active listening and have an appreciation for people's differences. It requires leaders to take action and cultivate a sturdy foundation to build meaningful relationships. As a leader who encourages connections, you will need to be aware of how to inspire each person in your program to be seen, heard, and valued. It will take intentionality on your part. Here are two strategies designed to help you implement uplift principle #1:

1. Schedule an individual "my moment" meeting.

This is a one-on-one scheduled session with each team member. The meetings are designed to celebrate what your team is doing well. They should be conducted by a designated supervisor and can be at least 5 to 10 minutes long. The supervisor's role during the meeting is to provide positive feedback for the tasks that the team member has done. These meetings can be scheduled monthly, quarterly, or as needed to uplift your team. Remember, this is not a

session to critique or criticize. This is their moment to be in the spotlight. Keep it positive and encouraging.

2. Block out time to spend in each classroom at least weekly to build connections.

When planning your monthly to-do list, build in time to visit each class to connect with your teachers and the children. For instance, you might block out Tuesday to do music and movement with infants and toddlers or Thursday to join preschool and Pre-K classrooms during outside time. As a director or administrator, every moment counts. Be flexible and use the entire month to block out time. In Chapter 6 it says, "A playful leader creates a joyful environment where creativity and connection thrive." Intentionally joining in play with your teachers and children can uplift them and you, too.

As a director, I built in time to visit the classrooms twice a week. I would have a day where I would read a book, do music and movement, facilitate an art activity, or join in play with all the age groups during choice time, starting with the infants and making my way to the pre-K classrooms. I was uplifted and encouraged to build connections through activities and conversations. The teachers and children enjoyed it. It allowed me to support my team by acting as their assistant teacher for a short time.

I know firsthand how finding time in your schedule can be a challenge. I would have my time planned out and have to pivot if someone called out, or if I was needed for center tours, unplanned parent meetings, unscheduled requested reports, or unplanned staff meetings. Blocking out time allowed me to see where I could move my schedule around if I needed to.

Adding "my moment" meetings and blocking time out to encourage connections within your program will take time. Start small by allocating or setting aside 1 hour a week, and increase your time when implementing these strategies. It will be worth it.

PAUSE AND REFLECT

- What barriers do you face when planning time to support teaching staff?
- Think about a time when you encouraged and connected with your team. Was it meaningful?

Uplift Principle #2: Inspire Open-Mindedness

Lynn Good, CEO, president, and chairman of the Board of Duke Energy is known for a quote that resonates with me very much: "If you keep an open mind, you can learn so much from the people around you" (Brainy Quote, n.d.). Open-mindedness is the ability to consider different beliefs, values, perspectives, ideas, and opinions without preconceived judgments or biases (Cherry, 2025). To truly be open-minded may be impossible, but you can strive to be open-minded by seeking to understand individuals that are not like you.

I have been managing and coaching in early childhood for over 20 years, and I genuinely thought I was an open-minded person until I began coaching. When I was managing a program as a director, the focus was on to-do checklists, productivity, and achieving desired outcomes set by the organization. Coaching individuals requires encouraging growth and development, collaborating, and taking the time to see their perspective. I will never forget my first observation while training during my transition from being a director to becoming a QRIS (quality rating improvement system) coach. My supervisor trained me to observe a classroom, along with how to provide the teachers with observation notes. I was excited to be able to support the teachers and children in this program. To my surprise, as we entered the classroom, it was very chaotic, and we witnessed many behavior challenges, and teachers displayed negative emotions of frustration. I could feel myself standing there but did not realize the facial expression I was giving until my supervisor approached me and whispered, "Fix your face." I responded back gently by saying, "What is wrong with my face?" She said, "Your face does not look supportive. It looks like you are passing judgment. We are here to support the teacher and keep an open mind." Shortly after, during our debrief, I explained that I had no idea that my face and body were sending unsupportive messages. I learned quickly that being a coach requires understanding that each program, classroom, and teacher is different and requires a coach to be supportive. It is important to have a lens of curiosity to explore what is going on by keeping an open mind to what you see and hear. Have you ever found yourself in a comparable situation?

After being a coach for a year, I was out conducting an observation in a toddler room, and my lens had changed. The room was chaotic, with crying toddlers ready for lunch, and none of the transition strategies were working. I smiled at the teacher and asked, "How can I support you?" She smiled and replied, "Can you check with the kitchen and find out why lunch is late?" I replied, "Absolutely." When I returned, they were on the carpet getting their wiggles out with music and movement, and the teacher and children were dancing and laughing. I communicated that the cook was running a little behind and that lunch would be there within 5 minutes. We danced with the kids, and before we knew it, lunch had arrived. I helped her with handwashing, and she began giving the toddlers their lunch when they arrived at the table. At the end of the observation, she thanked me, and I told her she did an awesome job. In my follow-up coaching email, I praised her again and conveyed that if she needed anything to support her, she could just ask me. I told her I was just an email away and looked forward to seeing her next month.

For uplift principle 2, inspire open-mindedness as a leader, consider these two strategies:

1. Take a step back.

Schedule time to observe and take notes on what you see in your program. For instance, during my coaching session in the toddler room the teacher needed support. By taking a step back, I could ask and respond in a way that the teacher needed to be successful and nurturing to her children.

2. Check your "anchoring bias."

Anchoring bias is a type of cognitive bias that causes people to automatically make judgments based on the first part of the information they receive to form an "opinion" (Krockow, 2019; Nikolopoulou, 2025). When entering your program or classrooms, take time to receive all the information to gain perspective before making any decisions about what you are seeing. I began to check my anchoring bias by assessing the situation and not jumping to conclusions based on what I saw. Having an open mind and asking questions allowed me to support the teachers and the children.

I wish I could tell you that I always used these two strategies and was absolutely perfect as a coach or director. It took time, and when I failed, I created a space to authentically reflect and make adjustments in my approach. By practicing open-mindedness, your team will be uplifted and inspired.

PAUSE AND REFLECT

- Can you recall a time when you took a step back to observe your program without judgment? If so, what did you observe?
- Do you consider yourself to be an open-minded person? Why or why not?

Uplift Principle #3: Choose to Care and Connect Through Challenges

When faced with challenges, it can be tricky to navigate and can leave one wondering if they made the right choice or if they managed to solve a problem correctly that was beneficial to all parties involved. Choosing to care for and connect with your team by developing solutions to a problem might be easy breezy for some of us and may cause anxiety, fear, and uneasiness if we do not like to mitigate concerns. When problems arise, creating a framework to fit the organization's culture is important. A handbook or the human resource department might have guided you or the administrative team on how to supervise staff with specific problems, for example, the policy and procedure for workplace bullying, violence in the workplace, safety, or code of conduct. These protocols within your organization are essential. The question I would like you to consider is: How do you choose and connect with your team through challenges that are meaningful to them?

I would like to introduce you to the "care circle" approach, which has been a key factor in uplifting the early childhood educators we lead. In 2020, during COVID-19, we noticed that the morale of the teachers in a professional learning program was low during our training sessions. We wanted to create an environment that would let them know they were not alone and ignite a sense of belonging among the Pre-K teachers. We called this part of the training "the teacher chat lounge." Later, our team renamed this "care circles." A "care circle" is defined as a group of individuals having meaningful discussions in a circle by reflecting on questions that are tied to the content of a training session, such as reflecting on self-care, or shared areas of concern to be addressed as a group (Byington, 2023). A "care circle" can be incorporated into a staff meeting, training session, or online meeting (platform of your choice). One online platform that we have used as a team is Zoom. Online "care circles" can be one large discussion group, or you can create break-out rooms with a maximum of four to five people.

Having a conversation in a circle is not new. This concept is rooted in Indigenous values and knowledge systems emphasizing interconnectedness and empowering each participant to share in a nonjudgmental environment known as a "talking circle" (Rieth, 2023). Humans have been talking in circles for centuries, and it is practiced formally and informally in organizations, education, and churches and among friends and families. Here are the steps for how to create your own "care circles" with teams:

1. Use reflective practices to determine the needs of the people you lead or care for to help you formulate your questions. Reflective practice is a cycle of continuous learning when educators take the time to stop, think, challenge, and change practices that can make a positive impact (Kennedy & Stonehouse, 2017). Use a maximum of three questions.
2. Set the ground rules.
    a. Use a visual timer to guide the conversation.
    b. One person speaks at a time. Stay on topic.
    c. Be respectful.
    d. You can share your story, but please do not share someone else's.
3. Allow up to 30 minutes for your "care circle" (about 10 minutes per question).
4. At a training session, meeting, or gathering take chairs and create mini-circles with no more than eight people per circle.
5. After each question, encourage participants to move around to other circles to make connections with other participants.
6. Present the question on a slide or read the question aloud.
7. At the end of the "care circle" check in with participants to ensure that it was a positive experience. Adjust as needed to support the growth of your team.

Iris's Approach

It was brought to Iris's attention that the staff had been complaining to one another about the changes she had implemented as the director of The Children's Garden. Iris had been working on changing the work environment to create a culture that cultivates uplifting others by building connections with her staff, children, and families. Iris knew she could not do this by herself, and it would take the buy-in of her administrative team first. She met with her assistant director, Pam, and administrative assistant, Rosa, to produce a plan after speaking with her two toddler teachers. Pam and Rosa were not shocked and were just as concerned as Iris. Pam and Rosa have worked for The Children's Garden childcare center for the last 8 years and had worked for a couple of directors. They explained to Iris that they would give her their full support. After much deliberation, they decided the first phase of the plan was to schedule a paid staff meeting with a heart theme titled "All We Need Is You." Iris explained that the number one goal of this staff meeting was to build connections and uplift the teachers. The staff meeting had a welcome atmosphere, with dinner and games, and implemented "care circles." The administrators praised the team on what they were doing well and opened the floor for the teachers to express any concerns they had. Some of the teachers expressed concerns about the name-to-face policy and how they did not think they needed to keep their counters free of clutter. The administration team was open to the information given and participated by validating with positive comments and questions for clarification. At the end of the meeting, they reviewed the uplift principles and introduced "care circles."

Iris: "During this portion of the staff meeting we would like to invite you to take part in "care circles." Pam, Rosa, and I have reflected on your concerns and how we can continue to support you. We have three questions on the PowerPoint to guide the conversation during this time. You will have 10 minutes of sharing before we move on to the next question. Pam will now share the ground rules."

Pam: "We will use a visual timer, so don't worry about the time. We will give you a 3-minute warning before moving to the next question. Be respectful by allowing one person to speak at a time."

Rosa: "We want this to be a safe place. You can share your story, but please don't share someone else's."

Iris: "After each question we will invite you to move around and find a new circle. Is there anything I can clarify?"

During the "care circles," Iris leaned in and was curious and open to what her teachers had to say.

Shannon: "I will read the first question. How does change make you feel?"

Jamal: "I must be honest. I do not like change. It makes me uncomfortable."

Mei: "It makes me feel anxious and excited at the same time."

Shannon: "As long as it is positive change, I am okay."

After 10 minutes of conversations, Iris spoke again.

Iris: "I love the conversations I am hearing. It is now time to find a new circle."

Rosa: "Here is your next question."

Jamal: "I can read this one. How can we support each other during this transition with the new changes being implemented?"

Alex: "It would be nice if we could just check-in on each other."

Jamal: "That's cool. We could also check in on Iris since she is new here."

Anna: "I agree. And maybe be more open-minded" (smiles).

The teachers continued to share their thoughts and insights.

Rosa: "It's time to switch circles for the last time."

Carla: "I can read the last question. What do you love about teaching?"

Shannon: "I love seeing my toddlers explore and learn. The expressions on their faces are priceless."

Maria: "I love connecting with the kids and their families."

It was heartwarming for Iris to hear the teachers' comments.

Iris: "Our 'care circles' have come to an end, and we hope that you have enjoyed them."

At the end of the meeting, Iris expressed her gratitude for their hard work and said she took notes and would set up times to speak with each of them during the next two weeks. She also asked them if they would be patient and come to her or her administration team if they had concerns that they would be willing to address. Iris and her administrative team felt good about the staff meeting and met on Monday to begin implementing the uplift principles. They also set up times to meet with each teacher for individual coaching sessions to discuss ideas, concerns, and their care circle experience. Iris and her administrative team were happy and grateful to uplift and create connections.

EXPERIENCING "CARE CIRCLES"

"Care circles" have become popular among our team and are used often. What I love about "care circles" is that they create a safe place for teachers to intentionally listen and be heard with no judgment. Even when obstacles remain, they feel cared for and supported by their team (Byington, 2023).

Below, you will find a few examples of early childhood educators' experiences with "care circles."

Personal Testimonies

Ms. Mayte—Nevada READY! Lead Pre-K Teacher

Care circles have been an absolute lifeline for me as an educator in early childhood development, offering much more than just professional support. They've been a source of emotional connection and understanding in both my work and personal life. In those safe, open spaces, I was able to share my struggles, doubts, and triumphs with fellow teachers, and more often than not, I realized that others were feeling the same way. Knowing that I wasn't alone in facing the challenges of managing a classroom, navigating complex relationships with children, or even juggling the demands of work and life, brought a deep sense of relief and comfort. The conversations weren't just about finding solutions; they were about creating an emotional bond, where we could share our vulnerabilities, lift each other up, and offer words of encouragement when things felt tough. There were moments when someone else's insight or experience gave me a breakthrough or provided a new way of thinking that I hadn't considered. These circles weren't just about becoming better teachers; they were about becoming better people, learning how to support and care for one another, and growing together in ways that made me feel more confident and whole, both in the classroom and beyond.

Ms. Tina—Nevada READY! Lead Pre-K Teacher

Teaching young children can be a very isolating experience. People who do not work in the field do not understand the stress we are under and seem to not really want to hear about it. People who do work in the field understand but want to tell their experiences and usually jump right over what you are saying. I understand it can be really freeing to finally speak with someone who goes through similar things that you are going through. I like care circles because I am with people who understand what the job requires. I don't have to explain it and get lost in translation. There is a clear speaker, and we are to listen and support that speaker by being heard. As I mentioned, it is a rarity for us. You listen to the person whether you are going through the same thing or not. This is different for us as well because we like to jump in with what is going on with us. When it is your turn the same is done for you. There is no judgment, just support and being heard. We are not always looking for problems to be solved, although that is ok too. Sometimes we just need to hear our words aloud. It may bring clarity to you or it may just give you a much-needed opportunity to unload and recharge.

Here are the key points these two teachers made about "care circles" that resonate with me:

- They are a source of emotional connection.
- They are a safe space.
- They create an emotional bond.
- Teachers uplift each other.
- They decrease isolation.
- They provide a judgment-free zone.
- They provide an opportunity to reflect and recharge.

PAUSE AND REFLECT

- How could you incorporate "care circles" into your organization?

Iris's Story Continued

Shannon and Mei were getting ready to go home and stopped by Iris's office. She invited them in, and they expressed how much happier they were and that they appreciated the time and effort she and the administrative team spent connecting with the team. They also reported how much laughing and fun they had with their peers since the staff meeting. Iris told them she was thankful they brought their concerns to her attention to begin the catalyst toward change. She said, "We are a work in progress, and I am happy about how much ground we have covered within these 3 months."

THE JOYFUL UPLIFT DIFFERENCE

Uplifting others by building connections supports your teaching teams, administration, children, and families and creates a space for growth and development. It is like harvesting a garden; through connections we make space for all to belong.

INDIVIDUAL REFLECTION

1. Reflect on how using "uplift principles" can build connections and uplift your team.
2. What policies or procedures do you have in place to create a safe place?
3. What does building connections and uplifting others mean to you?

BOOK OR GROUP DISCUSSION

1. What would be the potential outcomes of implementing "uplift principles" in your program?
2. How could "uplift principles" be applied to improve teacher–child interactions?
3. How can "care circles" become part of your program's workplace environment?

UPLIFT IN ACTION

Select one or more of the following to practice uplift in action.

- Schedule weekly "my moment" meetings.
- Block out time to build connections.
- Approach challenges with open-mindedness.
- Create "care circles" at your next staff meeting.
- Introduce "care circles" at your next parent engagement night.
- Block out time to join in play in your classrooms once a week.
- Create a resolution board in the staff lounge by allowing staff to post common concerns and let their peers provide solutions.

5

Creating an Uplifting Workplace

Danielle Pertile

THE MASTER GARDENERS

I am incredibly lucky to work on a campus that shares space with Master Gardeners, which is a horticultural education program offered through the University of Nevada, Reno. In addition to our office space, we have a large garden that spans multiple acres and is meticulously maintained by a group of hardworking professional gardeners and volunteers. This isn't just any old garden; we have roses, an herb and vegetable plot, a cactus grove, a fruit orchard, and

even a Zen rock garden. All in the heart of the Mohave desert! This space isn't just a testament to the master gardeners' skills in a harsh climate; it's an oasis for everyone who works in our office. The garden is bordered by a walking path and contains benches and picnic tables that invite employees and visitors to both literally and figuratively stop and smell the roses. Employees are often spotted taking their breaks or lunches out in the garden. I have even taken my laptop out to one of the picnic tables to work during nice spring days. It is true that our office would still function without these beautiful gardens, but having a joyful space available to us allows us to access the beauty, serenity, and peace it offers and through which it refreshes us for the rest of our workday.

PHYSICAL SPACE MAKES A DIFFERENCE

In the early childhood field, many classrooms are filled to the brim with vibrant visuals, soft and cozy resting spaces, intriguing play invitations, and varied sensory experiences that beg to be explored. Some classrooms lean toward neutral colors, natural items, and upcycled materials, while others display primary colors and bright, engaging toys. It is so exciting to visit new early childhood centers and classrooms and to see how the teachers and children represent their joy in the space!

As an early childhood leader, you have likely given a lot of thought to intentionally designing a welcoming, calming, and engaging space for children and their families. That first impression when a child and family walk into your center can be the deciding factor on whether the family chooses to enroll. What often ends up much lower on the priority list, however, is creating a welcoming and calming space for early childhood staff. Some childcare centers don't have a staff lounge (or break room), and if they do it can sometimes end up being more of a storage space than anything else. While most of this book focuses on the emotional and social environment of a childcare center, the physical space available to your staff should also be considered. This chapter will explore how, with some simple changes and additions, you can create an uplifting workplace environment for your staff outside the classroom.

Thoughtfully designed staff spaces are like well-planned gardens. A skilled gardener prepares the environment before planting, choosing between raised beds or ground soil, selecting the right nutrients, and considering sunlight, shade, and space. Some plants need a trellis to climb; others need room to sprawl. Similarly, as a leader, you must ask, what kind of environment will help your staff grow and thrive? What support, structure, and conditions will allow your team to truly bloom?

Iris's Story

As Iris began to settle more deeply into her position as director at The Children's Garden, she felt proud of the new practices she had implemented to uplift both herself and her staff. Though she knew she still had work to do, her regular staff meetings were more engaging, the classroom teams were beginning to collaborate with each other, and the children and families seemed more settled with the transition of leadership. Iris was beginning to see how the uplifting practices she had implemented were producing positive changes within her staff.

One afternoon, Iris left the center to pick up some snack supplies for an upcoming family event. As she walked out of the center to her car, she noticed one of her employees was eating lunch in their car. Iris smiled at her employee on her way out but didn't give it another thought as she became distracted by her errands. About an hour later, on her way back into the childcare center, arms loaded with overflowing grocery bags, she saw yet another employee sitting in their car, listening to music and texting while on their 15-minute break. This time, Iris's attention was caught. Why would employees spend their break times in their cars when they had a perfectly functional staff lounge? Iris knew that some of her staff may prefer the solitude of their cars, but still, she was curious.

Iris headed straight to the staff lounge with her grocery bags, as that was where those supplies would need to be stored until the event. She entered the room with fresh eyes, and considered it from the perspective of her staff members. What she had thought of as a usable space was dusty and cramped, filled with materials and art supply storage. The small kitchenette was hardly accessible because there were stacks of children's books and gallon bottles of paint and glue on the counter. The only seating available in the space was an old table and three chairs discarded by one of the classrooms, which were child-sized and uncomfortable for adults. Iris sighed. She usually ate lunch alone in her office and hadn't considered how unwelcoming this space had become. Iris decided to focus some energy and funding on creating a relaxing and inviting space for her staff, knowing this would be another important aspect to consider when it came to uplifting her team.

SETTING THE TONE

Author and designer Ingrid Fetell Lee has written extensively about how the physical space we're in can directly influence our joy, our productivity, and our overall moods. In her book, *Joyful: The Surprising Power of Ordinary Things to Create Extraordinary Happiness* (2018a), and in her TED Talk, "Where Joy Hides and How to Find It" (2018b), Lee describes the aspects of a joyful environment that, when implemented thoughtfully and intentionally in our living and workspaces, can uplift us throughout the day and bring new purpose to our work. In her TED Talk, she poses a question that deserves consideration: If a joyful physical space can uplift us and connect us more deeply to our work, why do we give it so little thought? As caregivers and educators, our primary focus is almost always on the children's experiences: their comfort, joy, and exploration. It's easy to overlook providing those same things for early childhood staff and, unfortunately, Iris's staff lounge example is all too common.

When early childhood center owners, directors, and administrators intentionally create warm, inviting, and joyful spaces for their staff, it can be so much more than just a cute space to eat lunch or take a break. Thoughtfully planned employee spaces can encourage staff collaboration, build trust within the team, and allow educators to recharge and care for their mental health (Atyah, 2020; Kokoros, 2023; Leung et al., 2006). These spaces are most often a staff lounge or break room, but can also include the lobby, offices, and even thoughtful touches in the staff restrooms. Early childhood education work can, at times, be mentally and physically draining as much as it is powerfully rewarding. Having an oasis outside the classroom to step into, even just for a few minutes of breathing and resetting, can build staff resilience. Creating uplifting spaces for staff sets the tone for an uplifted early childhood workforce.

GETTING OTHERS INVOLVED

Just as with implementing any other new teaching or leadership practice, there may be some trial and error involved when building uplifting spaces for your staff. If, like Iris's employees, educators are accustomed to taking their lunches or breaks out in their cars, it may take staff time to fully put the space to use. (It should also be noted that some team members may still prefer the quiet social break their cars can offer.) It is critical that leaders both get to know the employees in their center and invite them to be involved in the process of creating spaces for them (Kaiser Permanente, 2024). Without that input from the individuals for whom the room is designed, we are more likely to design a space that appeals to us and may not meet their needs.

For example, reading a good book and drinking a hot cup of black tea is what helps me feel refreshed, so my ideal staff space would have a shelf of interesting books and a kettle with mugs and tea bags. I also happen to know that one of my colleagues enjoys yoga and would love to have space to stretch and breathe during the day. Another loves her morning coffee and would likely feel disappointed if the only offering was a selection of teas. A third colleague has shared that creating art with paints or adult coloring pages is what helps her relax. Each of these items is a simple thing that could be added to a space to make it inclusive and welcoming to everyone.

Staff Input

Seeking staff input and getting to know what they like is essential. As you can see from the previous section, I am better able to support my team in ways that connect with them personally because time and effort have been spent to get to know them. One way to ensure that work and break spaces meet the needs of your staff is to learn more about their preferences, hobbies, and what helps them feel refreshed. Each time my department hires a new team member, they are invited to fill out a "getting to know you" questionnaire that prompts for simple information such as favorite treat, favorite color, hobbies, and even favorite scents (Byington, 2023). Our team uses the responses to prepare personalized surprises for birthdays or other celebrations.

It's not always possible to cater to every preference, especially when a large group of people are involved. A phrase that comes to my mind when I receive input from too many sources is *there are too many cooks in this kitchen!* However, it is possible to involve staff in planning without it becoming a too-many-cooks situation. You might consider creating a short survey for staff asking questions like "What helps you feel relaxed?" and "What do you do to recharge and refresh your mind and body?" These open-ended prompts will likely reveal patterns and similarities that you can then draw from when creating uplifting spaces. You can use the results of these surveys together with the results of the "getting to know you" questionnaire to create an uplifting space that is inclusive of the whole team. Collecting and using responses in this way allows everyone to share their thoughts and ideas but also helps you avoid becoming bogged down by trying to please everyone.

Another way to involve your team and get them excited about the updated space is to rotate small displays or bulletin boards in the staff space once a month. Instead of you choosing which joyful items, decorations, or artwork will be displayed, your staff take turns to put their uplifting spin on the space. Not only does this allow for creative expression within your staff, but it also lightens your load as a leader, and it helps you get to know your team even better. One staff member may choose to decorate with a butterfly theme for their month, while another may go with rainbows, and another may brighten up the space with plants. Providing a small monthly budget, if possible, will encourage your staff to participate and bring their joy into the space.

Involving Families

Families are often a helpful resource when working toward the goal of uplifting staff. Many families are willing to donate time, funds, or even their craftsmanship to celebrate and uplift the educators that support and guide their children every day. Many of the items or strategies in the following sections are ones for which you may be able to seek family support. You may have a grandfather who takes great pride in his garden and would be willing to donate an occasional bouquet, or a mother who bakes and would be happy to share something delicious with the staff once a month. Artistic family members might be willing to provide beautiful art for the staff lounge or to come decorate a bulletin board for staff shout-outs. Though not every family is able to donate funds, some are willing to chip in to provide a special treat or to help the center save up for a larger or more expensive item like a new coffee maker or comfy couch. Most families would love to offer their support however they can, and allowing them to do so not only uplifts your team but also strengthens the school–family community.

PAUSE AND REFLECT

- What helps you feel relaxed?
- What does your ideal staff lounge look and feel like?
- How might you be able to involve families in creating an uplifting workplace for your staff?

STRATEGIES FOR CREATING UPLIFTING STAFF SPACES

Now that you have spent some time reflecting on why and how you might involve others in creating relaxing and uplifting staff spaces, the following section will provide strategies that you might find helpful in doing just that. Some of the strategies in this section will be quick and free or low cost, while others may require more careful planning and budgeting. A few of the following strategies may be unrealistic for the space, time, and funds you have available to you. What is most important in the following ideas is that you are thoughtful and intentional in your uplifting work. Making any effort to create a peaceful and joyful space for your staff goes a long way in communicating that you appreciate them and that they are valued.

As we design uplifting staff spaces, let's take inspiration from a thoughtfully tended garden. Just as a thriving garden requires attention to different elements such as light, soil, water, and space, an uplifting environment for your team should nurture the senses, the mind, the body, and social connections. Uplifting the senses is like selecting the right mix of flowers and herbs; it means attending to your team's sensory needs and using calming sights, sounds, and textures to create a soothing atmosphere. Uplifting the mind mirrors the way a garden invites quiet reflection and curiosity; it includes providing opportunities for your staff to spark new ideas or simply rest their minds from the busy energy of the classroom. Uplifting the body is like ensuring plants get the right nutrients and room to grow; It involves offering moments for movement, comfort, and physical refreshment. Finally, uplifting accomplishments and social connections is the harvest, the time to celebrate growth, share successes, and cultivate a strong, collaborative team rooted in trust and joy.

1. Uplift the Senses

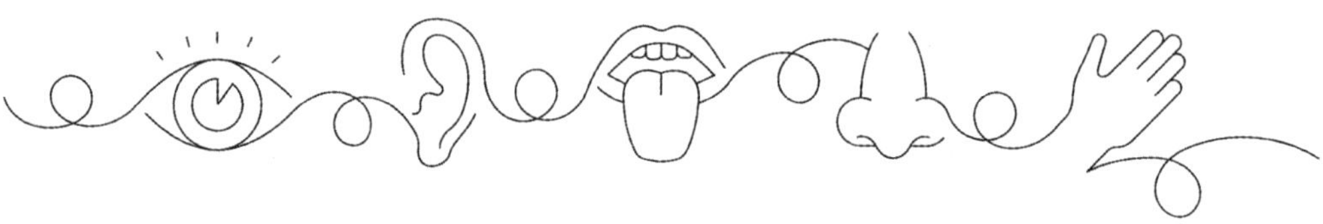

Just as plants respond to light, sound, and touch, we experience the world through our senses. Our eyes, ears, hands, and entire bodies help us process what's happening around us. In the hustle and bustle of an early childhood classroom, educators are often overwhelmed by constant sensory input. That's why an ideal staff space should offer a sensory break where the environment soothes rather than stimulates, giving staff a chance to reset and recharge.

Music

Though everyone has different tastes in music, music is generally something that everyone connects and responds to in their own way. Music can calm us and get us excited and motivated. Calming background music can help soothe educators who feel frazzled by their busy classrooms. Staff can even be involved in choosing the music if you are using a music streaming service.

Scents

Like music, scent preferences vary by person, but a small collection of scented lotions can provide a calming sensory experience for many educators. Certain scents like lavender and eucalyptus can be calming, while citrus scents are often invigorating.

Textures

To provide a visual and tactile break from the hectic classroom, provide materials of varying textures. Fluffy and soft pillows, woven baskets and placemats, and patterned rugs can create a texture-rich and relaxing space. Texture can even be added to the walls through art such as woven hangings, acrylic paintings, or children's nature or found object collages.

Fidgets

Fidgets can provide calming sensory input through repetitive motions. Researchers recommend caution in the use of fidget toys as learning tools for students because they sometimes become more of a distraction than a support during deep focus times (Kriescher et al., 2022). However, having simple, engaging fidgets in staff spaces allows educators to take a mental break and can encourage playfulness.

Greenery/Nature

Adding flowers, plants, or even nature prints (in fabrics or art on the walls) brings the calming power of nature indoors and creates a sense of freedom (Lee, 2018a). One childcare director brought in grass-like spider plant "babies" (small pieces of spider plants that grow directly from the larger plant and can be repotted to grow on their own) and made them available to take in the staff lounge. The educators brought them back to their classrooms and supported the children in caring for these low-maintenance plants. Having the same plant from the same source in each classroom helped create a deeper sense of unity within the childcare center. When those spider plants started producing their own baby plants, they were sent with children to care for at home with their families.

2. Uplift the Mind

Like a garden that grows and renews with each season, the field of early childhood is constantly evolving. Educators must keep their minds sharp and stay open to fresh ideas in order to provide the best care for children and families. A well-designed staff space supports this growth, offering fertile grounds for new thinking, inspiration, and even much-needed

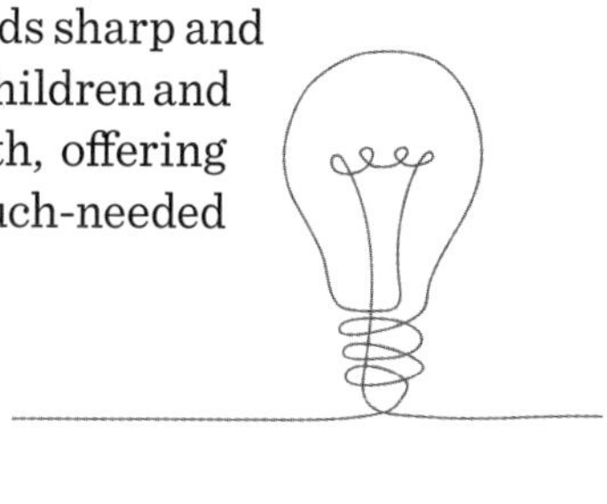

mental rest. Whether it's a place to reflect, learn, or simply pause, uplifting staff spaces help minds bloom.

Puzzles/Word Puzzles

For many people, puzzles (jigsaw puzzles, word puzzles, logic puzzles, etc.) are a way to focus the mind, practice creative problem-solving, and tune out the stress of the day. Building jigsaw puzzles with others also encourages teamwork and social connections.

A Computer for Online Staff Development

One way to uplift your staff is to provide tools and resources for them to complete professional development opportunities. By having a computer that is open for staff use, educators can complete online training and webinars, participate in online professional groups, and even research activity ideas for their classrooms.

Books

When I was teaching at a child development lab program in Las Vegas, I was amazed to walk into the staff break room on my first day and see a wall of books. Many were resource books we could use for inspiration or further professional development, and there were also copies of professional publications such as the National Association for the Education of Young Children's *Young Children* and *Teaching Young Children*. Having these resources available was helpful to me as I began my professional journey. In the office in which I work now, there is a shelf of novels and paperbacks (fiction and nonfiction) in the staff lounge that are available to take and replace, such as with little free libraries; take a book, leave a book.

For staff who enjoy reading for relaxation and enjoyment, having "fun reads" available can provide a sense of fun and help them recharge with a good story. For others who turn to resource books for ideas and inspiration, having current and interesting resource materials will help them grow their teaching practices.

Art

The acts of both viewing and creating art have been tied to positive mental health gains (Barker, 2019; Cacouris, 2022; Law et al., 2021). Art stimulates the mind and relaxes the senses. Creating art (through drawing, painting, sculpting, or even photography) builds creativity. Simple art materials can be provided in staff spaces, such as adult coloring books and colored pencils, watercolors, clay, or even crayons and markers. Art created by staff, families, or even leadership can be hung on the walls in any staff space. Additionally, you could hang art prints on the walls to encourage relaxation and creativity.

Figure 5.1. Canvases created during a team retreat.

During a team retreat, small square canvases, paint, and brushes were provided to each team member, and everyone was instructed to paint a specific letter using whatever colors or styles appealed to them. When the project was completed, our team had spelled out "Intentionality," which was our team word for the year. The canvases were hung on the wall in our staff space to remind us of our team word for the year and our fun community-building project (see Figure 5.1).

3. Uplift the Body

Just as every plant needs the right conditions to thrive—some needing rest in the shade, others reaching for the sun—every educator has unique physical needs. The demands of classroom work can take a real physical toll, so an uplifting staff space should offer supportive, comfortable furniture that invites rest and restoration. For some, gentle movement like stretching or a brief walk can be just the refresh they need to return feeling renewed, much like a garden revives after the rain.

Adult-Sized Furniture

Like Iris, I have walked into staff spaces at childcare centers in which the only available seating is child-sized. This sent a message to me that the comfort of the staff wasn't much of a priority. During one site visit, an educator told me that she never used the room because it was so uncomfortable. One of the first steps of refreshing any staff space is to assess the furniture and ensure that the seating and tables are both adult-sized and in good condition (Kokoros, 2023).

In the last few years, many classrooms have begun incorporating flexible seating, which is a way to honor differing needs and learning preferences. For a staff room, you might consider bringing in some beanbags or exercise balls to allow staff to choose what is most comfortable for them.

Yoga Mats

Many people feel refreshed and renewed through exercise, and exercise is a self-care practice (Mu et al., 2024). While it might be unrealistic to provide large exercise equipment like a treadmill, having a couple of yoga mats available (and space to use them) creates an opportunity for staff to stretch, practice their mindful

breathing, and recharge during their break times. Cleaning supplies should also be made available so staff can wipe the mats down after use, or staff may choose to bring their own mats.

Food and Drinks

Providing snacks and drinks is one of the most common ways I see childcare leaders uplifting their staff. Surprising the team with a pizza lunch once a month or bringing in a staff member's favorite coffee or candy treat for their birthday is a simple way to acknowledge staff and create connections within the team. In staff spaces, you might consider providing a selection of tea bags, coffee pods, and assorted snacks such as granola bars, trail mix, and chips if possible.

4. Uplift Social Connections by Celebrating Accomplishments

Just as a thriving garden flourishes through diversity and mutual support, a strong team grows through recognition and connection. Leaders can cultivate an uplifting environment by celebrating each team member's unique strengths and accomplishments, much like honoring the distinct beauty of every bloom. By fostering social connections, encouraging collaboration, and nurturing trust, you help your team grow together, rooted in shared purpose and collective success (Hylton & Vu, 2019).

Win Board

At the Spiral Up Academy, a training program for new hires in early childhood, all participants are provided with a workbook that provides detailed note prompts to guide them through the weekly training and coaching sessions. At the back of the workbook is a blank page titled "Win Board." Whenever a participant feels they've made a breakthrough, no matter how small, the coaches prompt them to write it on their win board. Sometimes, the coaches catch those small wins that participants miss as well! Examples include, "I set up an activity that kept children engaged through the whole play time!" or "I got the children ready and out to the playground exactly on time today." Over time, the win board fills up with accomplishments large and small, and participants can look back on them when they need a reminder about why they do this work.

You can incorporate a staff win board using a bulletin or poster board in your staff space. Provide pens or markers and brightly colored sticky notes or paper cutouts that follow a monthly theme (for example, snowflakes cutouts in January or daisy cutouts in April). When staff feel they've had a win in the classroom, they can write it down and hang it on the win board. Staff and leadership can also write wins for others based on their observations, such as "Gemma led an awesome play dough sculpture activity today!" This practice encourages staff to celebrate themselves and others.

Superpower Strengths

Our team recently used this activity during an all-team meeting. We sat in a circle, and each of us was given a superhero bulletin board cutout. We wrote our names on the front and then passed them around the circle. As our superhero journeyed around the circle, each team member wrote a "superpower" for that person on the back of the cutout. When my little hero returned to me, I saw words such as "intentional," "motivated," and "passionate" written on it. This was such an uplifting and encouraging activity for our team! When finished with the superheroes, you can hang them in staff spaces to remind your team of their super strengths. Another option is to encourage the team to keep their superheroes in their classrooms so they can revisit their superpowers whenever they like.

Uplift Sprinkles

As I wrote in Chapter 2, uplift sprinkles are a fun and meaningful way to collect uplifting moments in your work and interactions. For an uplifting staff space, uplift sprinkles may be a basket or jar in which staff write and collect children's funny sayings, joyful classroom moments, or inspiring quotes. Whenever someone needs a laugh or inspiration, they can pull an uplift sprinkle from the jar and read it.

Positive Descriptive Feedback

A powerful way to support and uplift best practices in the classroom is to conduct observations and provide meaningful feedback. You can incorporate this into staff spaces by creating a board of positive descriptive feedback. You may also use photos you take in the classroom to highlight the work. An example might be "Ms. Shronda supported children in measuring their block towers and charting the results" alongside a photo of the activity. These practices help staff feel seen and valued and encourage continued best practice in the classroom.

Word Cloud

When one new member joined our team recently, she shared that the families and staff at her previous school had given her a printed word cloud as a parting gift before she moved on. This word cloud had her name in the middle and was populated with words generated by the staff and families. "Kind," "caring," "present," and "confident" were some of the words in her word cloud, and she shared that it was such a meaningful gift. There are many free word cloud generators online. It would be an easy and low-cost way to add encouragement to staff spaces and another great way to get families involved in uplifting your staff.

Birthday/Accomplishment Decorations

Childcare centers might not always have a budget for birthday or accomplishment celebrations for each team member, but you can uplift your staff with small gestures in staff spaces. Hanging balloons or a banner made by the children can brighten up the space. Small, thoughtful treats can brighten someone's day. An educator with whom I worked discovered that her classroom team had hidden packages of her favorite gum all over the school for her to find on her birthday one year. She found packs of gum in her staff locker and mailbox, in the staff lounge, by the staff computer, in the fridge, and even taped to her classroom door! She was so excited about the gesture, the adventure, and the surprise of finding her favorite treat in unexpected places.

Iris's Approach

Iris enlisted a few classroom family members to volunteer some time, and with their help the staff lounge was cleaned and organized in one day. One family donated a gently used couch, and Iris was able to purchase an adult-sized table and chairs. She accessorized the space with colorful art prints and asked some artistically inclined staff members to donate a few pieces as well. Iris solicited feedback from her staff about what practices and items help them feel refreshed, and through family donations and a small budget from the center, she was able to provide a selection of snacks and drinks, scented lotions, and a few coloring books and puzzles for staff to enjoy during their time off.

Each classroom team was also assigned a month and given a small budget to decorate the table outside the staff lounge. The teams were so creative; they bought small decorations and incorporated children's art and projects into the décor. Each month, the classroom teams tried to outdo the decorations from the month before, and it became exciting for everyone to see what would appear next!

Slowly but surely, the team began to use the staff lounge more, and the room became a focal point for staff collaboration and connection. After a few months, Iris would step in to heat up her lunch (she tried to eat her lunch in the staff lounge at least twice a week to connect with staff) and would hear a conversation between team members about supporting a child experiencing a hard time or planning engaging play and art activities together. Iris was happy to see that the time and effort she had put in to create a space that would uplift her staff was doing just that.

THE JOYFUL UPLIFT DIFFERENCE

Creating an uplifting staff space, like cultivating a garden, takes time, care, and intention. It may require planning, effort, and occasionally some funding, but the payoff is a space where your team feels valued, refreshed, and even sparked by a sense of playfulness. Just as a garden offers renewal and connection, a well-designed staff space can become a catalyst for collaboration, joy, and professional growth. We are often deeply intentional about crafting welcoming, enriching environments for children and families, and our staff deserve that same thoughtful attention. Early childhood work is both rewarding and demanding, and a calming, inviting break space can offer the restoration needed to keep doing this important work with energy and heart.

INDIVIDUAL REFLECTION

1. Think of a time when your surroundings helped you feel refreshed and renewed. What made that space special for you?
2. What ways can you involve your staff in creating a welcoming space for them?
3. Think of one practice that you feel uplifts your
    a. Senses
    b. Mind
    c. Body
    d. Social connections

BOOK GROUP OR DISCUSSION QUESTIONS

1. How have you involved families in uplifting your staff, or what is one practice you will implement to involve families in uplifting your staff?
2. What practices have you used to uplift your team's accomplishments and their social connections with each other?
3. What is one way your staff (either individually or in groups) can be involved in designing the staff space?

UPLIFT IN ACTION

Select one or more actions to start creating an uplifting workspace.

- Write down a list of all available staff spaces. This might be a staff lounge, a staff bathroom, a kitchen, or an office.
- Create a survey for your team to find out what they might need or enjoy in a staff space.
- Write a list of uplifting items families may be able to donate.
- Set aside a small budget for staff to use to decorate the staff space.

6

Uplifting Others by Being Playful

Teresa Byington

When I was young, one of my favorite activities was playing outside with my siblings and friends. There were so many trees to climb and places to explore. We also loved to play games. Some of our favorite games were hide and seek, kick the can, and red rover, red rover. We played for hours or until the sun went down and our parents called us inside. As I grew up, play began to be replaced by other "important" activities that included homework and working at a variety of odd jobs. The magic and wonder of childhood became a distant memory. When I had my own children, I began to rediscover my playful side as I played with my children at home and in the park. It was enjoyable to run and laugh and play. Think about what you enjoyed doing as a child. What things do you enjoy doing now? Are you still being playful?

THE SCIENCE OF PLAY

According to psychiatrist Dr. Stuart Brown, author of the book *Play*, "play is a basic human need as essential to our well-being as sleep" (Brown & Vaughan, 2009). Play is a freely chosen activity that engages the mind and body and fosters curiosity, imagination, and critical thinking. Children explore the world through play. It is a foundation for learning. Children are more likely to develop a love of learning when they participate in play-based learning experiences. Play is also essential for adults. Miriam Beloglovsky, author of the book *Just Play: Inspiring Adult Play in Early Childhood Education*, states, "Play is crucial in adulthood because it fosters adaptiveness, creativity, role rehearsal, and mind-body integration" (Beloglovsky, 2023).

Playfulness is a powerful tool for uplifting, energizing, and inspiring early childhood educators. A playful leader creates a joyful environment where creativity and connection thrive. Play can strengthen relationships and foster resilience among staff. There are many benefits to being more playful for both you and the teachers, children, and families within your program. These benefits include making learning more engaging, building stronger bonds, and reducing stress and burnout. A playful approach can create a positive atmosphere where everyone can feel free to be themselves and uplift others.

WHY PLAYFULNESS UPLIFTS OTHERS

Play is contagious. When one person is playful, it encourages others to engage with joy. Joyful engagement leads to laughter and fun. When we laugh and play, we release endorphins (chemical in your body), which help us feel good. Play helps to create new neural pathways, boosting cognitive flexibility and critical thinking skills. Play is a language of connection that can transform relationships and enhance our well-being. Dr. Stuart Brown, founder of the National Institute of Play, discovered that play reduces stress by lowering cortisol (the stress hormone) and increasing dopamine, which improves mood and motivation (Brown & Vaughan, 2009). More playful individuals were found to maintain better health and experience greater happiness than their less playful counterparts in a study by Proyer and Brauer (2024a).

Being playful as an adult can have a significant role in coping with stress and contribute to life satisfaction (Proyer & Brauer, 2024b). Play also encourages divergent thinking, sparking innovative solutions to challenges. When employees are given the opportunity to play, they increase their productivity, engagement, and morale (Brown & Vaughan, 2009). Play and playfulness are essential strengths that contribute to adults' ability to thrive, find meaning, and make emotional connections in their lives (Guitard et al., 2024). Playfulness can act as an effective facilitator in reducing perceived stress and decreasing negative emotions. As a leader, your attitude sets the tone. When you embrace playfulness, you give permission to others to do the same.

PAUSE AND REFLECT

- How has playfulness uplifted you?
- How can you be more playful?

CREATING A PLAYFUL WORKPLACE CULTURE: SOW THE SEEDS OF PLAY

Leaders plant the seeds of a joyful, playful culture. Just as gardeners select the right seeds, leaders can intentionally embed play into their values and practices by modeling curiosity, inviting laughter, and giving others permission to experiment and explore. If you are struggling to be playful, schedule time to play every day. Play a game, dance to music, or engage in a creative outlet. Infuse play into your work and learning environments. When leaders play, they model a culture of joy and creativity for their teams. After I began focusing on joy, my leadership was transformed, and the playfulness within my team increased significantly. We played interactive games during team meetings; we added sensory items and fidgets to meetings and training sessions, and we looked for opportunities to increase the fun factor in our work. As my leadership evolved, my training style was positively impacted and my ability to make meaningful connections with others improved. As we played together, we formed closer bonds and team members look forward to coming to work.

It is important to recognize that play will look different for everyone. Some people may be uncomfortable being playful. Including reserved individuals in playful or team-building activities requires thoughtful design and sensitivity to different social comfort levels. It can be helpful to broaden the definition of playfulness to include quiet and creative activities such as collaborative puzzles and drawing challenges. Be sensitive to team members' comfort levels and allow them to choose their level of involvement without pressure. Use language that invites individuals to participate. Introverts may feel more comfortable in one-on-one and small-group settings. Consider including asynchronous play activities that do not require real-time interaction, such as contributing to a shared joy wall of photos or quotes. Normalize different styles of engagement and privately ask team members about the kinds of activities they would enjoy the most and what can be done to make play comfortable for all.

Nurture With Playful Practices

A garden needs water and sunlight. Play can nourish relationships. Water your team with moments of lightness and joy. What could you do to create a more playful environment for children and educators? Could you add creative play breaks for your team by setting up a doodle station in your break room or adding sensory play areas with kinetic sand? It can be very calming and relaxing to play with kinetic sand. Leaders can model playful interactions by using humor and surprise. Wear a funny hat or themed outfit on random days. Use silly voices or puppets to make announcements, host play nights where educators and families engage in a variety of games and playful activities.

Let Play Blossom in Your Community

Play fosters belonging. Leaders who encourage childlike wonder and promote joyful experiences help families feel seen and safe. Some families rarely play together for a variety of reasons. Other families may have the mindset that adults work and children play with children, not with adults. In one of the programs I oversaw, we held family events and modeled ways to play with children. It was interesting to see the gradual shift as the families began to engage in more playful interactions. The children's eyes lit up as they played with their families. Play began to blossom in this community.

Families and educators may also have conflicting viewpoints about different types of play, such as big body play or physical contact play. From a developmental perspective, big body play supports gross motor skills, body awareness, and self-regulation and can help children learn limits and boundaries through active, physical interaction. However, some educators may feel uneasy due to fears of injury, misinterpretation of aggression, or cultural expectations around appropriate behavior. Balancing these perspectives requires thoughtful policies, open communication with families, and professional development that equips teachers to distinguish between healthy roughhousing and unsafe behavior. When managed intentionally, with proper supervision and clear guidelines, big body play can be a safe and beneficial part of a child's learning experience. Be sensitive to concerns and encourage open discussions to promote a positive playful environment for everyone.

Pollinate Playfulness

Just like bees and butterflies bring life to a garden, leaders can bring energy and playfulness to the workplace. Playfulness encourages laughter and spontaneity. It can inspire free expression and imaginative play. Play can build trust, bonding and community building, and a sense of belonging. Use playfulness to strengthen relationships. Our team went on a scavenger hunt that required creative brainstorming. We laughed as we attempted to solve puzzles to discover clues. Win or lose, this shared experience created closer bonds among our team members.

It is important to remember that not everyone defines play and fun the same way. What kind of play is joyful for you? According to Catherine Price, author of *The Power of Fun*, having true fun requires three main ingredients:

1. Playfulness, or having a light-hearted spirit
2. Connection, or having a shared experience with someone else

3. Flow, or being totally engrossed and actively focused on the activity or the experience

Creating an environment that fosters playfulness, connection, and flow can significantly increase the fun factor for early childhood leaders and educators. Next, we will explore what the three main elements of true fun (playfulness, connection, and flow) might look like in an early childhood center.

Iris's Story

Iris was striving to add more playfulness to her childcare center to strengthen her relationship with her team. She had invited her team for a quick morning chat and snack before the children arrived. As the teachers entered the room, Iris greeted them wearing a big silly hat adorned with colorful flowers. She said in a sophisticated voice, "My name is Lady Bloom, and today is Silly Hat Friday. Everyone is invited to select one of the hats on the table to wear. You have permission to be as silly as your hat with your voice and actions. You can even give yourself a new name. Select a hat and then you will be invited to introduce yourself." The educators laughed as they tried on the different hats. Then they began introducing themselves.

Shannon selected a yellow striped hat with antennae and buzzed, "Welcome to my hive, I'm Ms. Busy Bee and I will be busy buzzing around today being as sweet as honey."

Jamal picked up a large popcorn bucket, placed it on his head, and said, "I'm Professor Popcorn. You are invited to pop into my class where I will be sharing stories on the adventures of Professor Popcorn and his trusty dog Kernel."

Everyone laughed with delight, and the staff got into a playful spirit. Several educators later shared how much fun they had with the children that day. Jamal wanted to know if he could wear a silly hat every Friday.

Connection

Connection can be found through collaborative play and spending time together. Meaningful conversations and sharing your interests with others can strengthen relationships.

During a classroom observation, Iris noticed a shy child sitting alone in the reading corner, clutching a favorite storybook but not engaging with the other children. Instead of approaching directly, Iris picked up a similar book and sat nearby, quietly turning the pages. After a few moments, she softly mentioned how much she enjoyed the illustrations in her book and wondered aloud about the child's storybook. The shy child looked up and, after some hesitation, shared the title of her book. Iris smiled warmly and asked what the child's favorite part of the book was, encouraging her to share her thoughts. Slowly, the child opened up, and Iris listened attentively, validating her feelings and showing genuine interest.

Flow

A person experiences flow when they become completely immersed in an experience, losing track of time and becoming so engaged and present in what they are doing that everyone else fades away. Flow is often found through creative sensory exploration or in nature. You may have experienced flow when you were dancing freely to music, creating a painting, playing a sport, or exploring the natural world.

Once a week, Iris taught a class in the art room so that teachers could have planning time. Before the children arrived, she dimmed the lights and set up individual art stations with watercolor palettes, brushes, and blank sheets of paper. When the small group of children arrived, Iris warmly welcomed them.

Iris said, "Today you are invited to use your imagination. Express yourself as you paint. I am going to play some music, and before we start painting, I want you to close your eyes and listen to the music. How does the music make you feel? What images do you see in your mind? Let the music guide your painting. Open your eyes and go to one of the art stations."

The children moved to the art stations and began painting. She noticed Olivia swaying to the music as she painted, and Leon was humming with the music. The children became involved in the painting as time dissolved and they were in the flow, expressing themselves freely.

PAUSE AND REFLECT

- What could you do to create a more playful workplace culture?
- How could you include more playfulness, connection, and flow in your work?

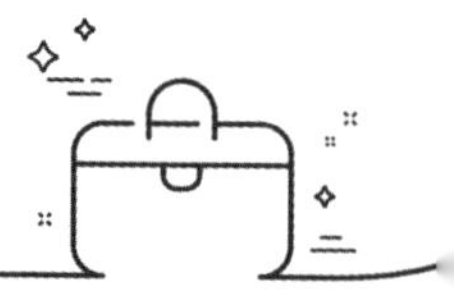

PLAYFUL LEADERSHIP TOOLKIT: LET THE SUNSHINE IN

Sunshine helps everything bloom. Leaders can shine joy through their own energy and openness. You can uplift the individuals you lead by adding playful leadership to your leadership style. Does that mean you need to be playful all the time? No, there are times to be serious and times to play. One idea is to create a playful leadership toolkit that can help you infuse more playfulness into your work, foster an uplifting environment, and enhance staff well-being. Here are some ideas:

Recognition and Celebrations

- Create playful awards to give to your team, such as The Smile Maker award for an educator with a contagious smile and positivity or the Early Morning Energizer award for an educator who greets the day with enthusiasm and motivates others to start their day strong. One of our team members greeted everyone in the morning by singing a song. She could be given the Sunshine Serenader Award!

- Initiate random surprise celebrations such as a surprise snack attack featuring favorite foods such as a popcorn bar or hot chocolate station for unexpected moments of food and fun.
- Pass out mystery thank-you notes expressing appreciation for team members' unique contributions. Place the notes in unexpected places such as on a child's chair or under the classroom door.
- Dedicate a day to random acts of kindness, where everyone is invited to surprise other team members with small gestures of kindness such as a flower, note, or treat.
- Create a thank you video or slideshow with clips and photos of children and families expressing thanks and appreciation for the educators' hard work. Seeing the impact of their work through heartfelt messages can let educators know they are appreciated.

Creativity and Innovation

- Set up play boxes with toys, loose parts, coloring materials, puzzles, and other items for team members to engage in during breaks.
- Add laughter yoga to your day by announcing that at a designated time, everyone needs to freeze and make their best yoga poses in the classroom without laughing. Telling someone not to laugh is often the surest way to get someone to laugh.
- Invite your team on a "walk and wonder." As you walk together outdoors, observe like a child. Ask yourself, "If I were a child, what would I notice? What sparks my curiosity? What creative ways could I engage children in the outdoors?" Work together to plan some creative outdoor activities for the children.
- Give your team prompts to promote innovation, such as "Create a game using bubbles, string, and music" or "Invent a classroom job that doesn't exist yet but would bring joy and purpose to the children." You could also challenge your team to be creative and teach a concept without using any words.

Playful Communication

- Uplift your team by adding some lightheartedness to your emails by adding fun GIFs, emojis, or witty subject lines such as "Fun Friday Forecast." One of my team members created personalized birthday wishes that were sent to each person on our team on their birthday. Each wish included a visual of something that the person finds joyful such as sunshine, rainbows, hummingbirds, butterflies, or watermelon.

- Ask certain team members to engage in a secret mission, such as "You are invited to send someone a text with a photo of something they would find joyful." One of my team members often sends me texts of things they saw that they think I will find joyful, such as a bird with colorful feathers or peacocks she saw on vacation at a zoo in Louisiana. She said, "The birds made me think of you." Very joyful!
- Host friendly competitions such as trivia games, scavenger hunts, or team challenges to energize staff. At our office in December, someone hid an Elf on the Shelf somewhere in the building, and the first person to find it and send in a photo received a small prize.

Lead With Playful Energy and Mindset

- Be playful yourself. Set the tone by using positive humor, showing curiosity, and embracing the playful aspects of your leadership. One of my favorite things to do is to dress up in themed outfits when I am giving presentations. I have been Chef Teresa, Pilot Byington, Coach T, The Great and Powerful Storyteller (Wizard of Oz), Indiana (Jones) Byington, Professor Plum, and a camp counselor. It always brings smiles to my team when I show up in one of these creative outfits. In fact, several of my team members are also willing to dress up during themed presentations!
- Model joyful leadership by bringing optimism and resilience to your work. Playful approaches can often help your team navigate obstacles with a positive mindset. Our annual Celebration of Joy and Friendship has included time to play games, learn the salsa, paint, and do some joyspotting by noticing joyful things in our surroundings.

Playful Reflection

- Create a set of playfulness reflection cards with prompts such as "What is something fun you did this week?" or "What is one way you can add more joy to your work tomorrow?"
- Keep a journal and reflect on how you brought playfulness into your leadership. Write about what went well and how it impacted your team. This can help you be more intentional about including play in your leadership.
- Create a calendar with weekly playful prompts. For example, week 1: Share a story that makes you laugh with the children; week 2: Take a 5-minute dance break with the children; week 3: Wear your favorite silly socks; week 4: Play a new game every day.

PAUSE AND REFLECT

- What playful leadership ideas would you like to add to your playful leadership toolkit?
- How could you lead with a more playful mindset?

OVERCOMING BARRIERS: ALLOW SPACE FOR GROWTH

Gardeners often encounter weeds and rocks in their gardens that need to be removed. They carefully eradicate these obstacles to allow space for growth. Likewise, leaders will face barriers that will need to be overcome. By tending to the environment with intention, growth is possible. Remember that infusing playfulness into your work can bring joy and engagement and uplift others, but it will take time and commitment to allow space for growth. Here are some potential barriers and how you can overcome them.

Resistance: Some educators or administrators may view playfulness as unprofessional or a distraction from serious work. They may not see the value and view it as unnecessary or have concerns that it will negatively affect productivity.

- Potential solutions: Tie play to outcomes by showing how play improves engagement, problem-solving, and team cohesion. Share success stories. Model playfulness yourself as the leader to show it is acceptable and encouraged. Start small with lower-risk playful activities and acknowledge concerns.

Time constraints and workload: With demanding schedules, adding playfulness may feel like adding another thing to your already full workload.

- Potential solutions: Seek ways to integrate playfulness into daily routines, such as adding playful songs or silly movement to transition times. Use micro-play strategies such as fun greetings or quick dance breaks to bring in elements of playfulness. Encourage play-based self-care by placing fidget toys or puzzles in the break rooms. Ask for volunteers to help initiate the playful activities.

Fear of judgment or looking unprofessional: You may be hesitant to be playful for fear of being perceived as silly, immature, or unprofessional.

- Potential solutions: Seek to normalize playfulness in professional settings by showing how creativity, humor, and lightheartedness can improve morale and effectiveness. Reframe play as a leadership strength that can boost innovation and engagement. Provide examples of respected professionals using play, such as Ms. Rachel, Tabitha Brown from the TV show *Tab Time,* and Fred Rogers from *Mister*

Rogers' Neighborhood. Encourage a judgment-free environment by celebrating any efforts to be playful.

Cultural and personal differences in playfulness: Not everyone will express playfulness in the same way. There will be cultural and personal differences that can impact how comfortable people feel about engaging in playful activities.

- Potential solutions: Offer a variety of playful options that include hands-on creativity and problem-solving games. Respect individual comfort levels and encourage involvement within a safe, low-pressure environment. Keep playfulness inclusive and adaptable and be mindful of different perspectives. Let each person choose their own unique and personal playful approach.

Impact of childhood trauma: Individuals that have experienced childhood trauma or chronic stress often have psychological defenses that inhibit their ability to engage in playful or joyful experiences. Childhood trauma can disrupt the development of brain regions responsible for emotional regulation and safety perception. Adults with trauma histories may struggle to feel safe enough to let go and play or experience guilt and discomfort when engaging in joyful activities. Some adults may not have a mental model for what healthy, joyful play looks like.

- Potential solutions: Encourage individuals to start with small, low-risk activities and gradually increase exposure to playful experiences. Create environments where play is guided and supported; use music to guide spontaneous movement. Gentle movements such as dance or yoga can help individuals reconnect with joyful playfulness. Let children lead, and follow their cues to build confidence in engaging in playful interactions.

Balancing playfulness with structure: Some educators may worry that too much playfulness will lead to a lack of discipline, routines, or focus on the classroom or workplace.

- Potential solutions: Use intentional playfulness. Play doesn't mean chaos. Structured playful activities can keep engagement high while also maintaining focus. Set clear expectations about what is appropriate. Combine playfulness with your learning objectives. Use playful transitions to keep structure intact.

Managing skeptical families or stakeholders: Some families or administrators may question the value of playfulness in a professional setting, believing it takes away from academics or efficiency.

- Potential solutions: Educate stakeholders and families on the benefits of play and how it supports cognitive development and emotional intelligence. Invite families and others to see playful learning and engagement in action. Use language they value, such as "We are engaging in interactive learning strategies" or "We are fostering creativity and innovation." Provide examples of how playfulness has improved morale, engagement, or problem-solving in the classroom and organization.

Overcoming challenges to infusing playfulness requires intentionality and thoughtful leadership. Be purposeful so that play enhances the learning environment.

Implementation Tips

1. **Start small:** Begin with one or two activities, and then gradually add more playful elements to your leadership.
2. **Be consistent:** Play will become part of your workplace culture if you regularly include it in your work as a leader through daily actions.
3. **Lead by example:** Model playful behaviors and participate with your team when they engage in playful behaviors. Let your team know that you value their efforts.
4. **Ask for feedback:** Invite your team to give feedback on what activities they enjoyed the most and focus on those activities. Feedback can be obtained from an anonymous survey or during meetings and one-on-one conversations.

Playfulness isn't just about having fun; it is a leadership tool that can foster resilience. Play can be a buffer against burnout. Introducing playful stress-relief techniques (breathing exercises or impromptu stretching breaks) can help staff reset and recharge. Encouraging a playful mindset of finding joy even during challenges fosters adaptability and emotional well-being. By incorporating play into your leadership, you will uplift and empower your team to bring their best selves to work.

PAUSE AND REFLECT

- What challenges might you face to infusing more playfulness into your work?
- How could you overcome these challenges?

CONFLICTING PERSPECTIVES ON PLAY IN THE CLASSROOM

Alex and Maria were the pre-kindergarten teachers at The Children's Garden. Alex was a mindful educator. He was reflective. His demeanor fostered a sense of stability and safety. He approached each day with patience and intentionality. Alex was attuned to the needs of each student, helping them develop self-awareness and emotional regulation through gentle guidance and reflective practices. Alex started each day with calming routines that included morning stretches, breathing exercises and quiet moments of reflection. At the end of the day, he had the children practice gratitude and share something for which they were thankful.

Maria was a playful educator. Her strength was bringing elements of playful fun to each learning experience. She was energetic and loved to actively play games with children. Maria liked to incorporate movements and actions into learning through music and dance. She wanted learning to be an exciting adventure. She brought a creative and fun approach to the classroom.

Alex's and Maria's energy levels and approaches to teaching were very different. Usually their strengths complemented each other, but sometimes their differences could lead to conflicts. Maria loved to dream up new possibilities and often envisioned innovative ways to enhance the learning environment. In contrast, Alex was highly reflective and often analyzed past experiences to improve future outcomes. He valued structure and consistency over constant experimentation. Alex focused on what worked, preferring to use established strategies that had proven to be effective, while Maria had been pushing for more innovation and creativity in the daily schedule.

Maria's and Alex's differing perspectives on creative play versus consistent routines had led to ongoing arguments about how to best plan learning experiences and manage the classroom environment. Tension had been building, and Iris, the director at The Children's Garden, had determined that it was time to intervene. While each teacher brought valuable strengths to the team, their different perspectives and approaches had been hindering their ability to collaborate effectively.

PAUSE AND REFLECT

- If you were the leader of these two educators, what would you do?

When conflicts arise, it is important to encourage open dialogue and listen to team members to understand their perspective. One approach is to use play-based conflict resolution techniques. Here are some steps to follow:

1. **Observe first:** Watch and listen before stepping in. Look for underlying themes such as communication gaps, role confusion, or unmet needs. Determine whether the conflict is a one-time event or ongoing struggle.
2. **Approach with curiosity and neutrality:** Join the conversation calmly and respectfully. Use nonblaming language: "I noticed some tension during cleanup time. Can we talk about what was happening?"
3. **Make space for each voice:** Use props, metaphors, or visuals to externalize the problem and reduce personal defensiveness. Use playful tools such as loose parts to explore perspectives such as building a model to represent how they are feeling.
4. **Identify the core issue together:** Reflect and share what you hear without judgment. "It sounds like Maria values spontaneity and Alex needs consistency; however, both of you value school readiness."
5. **Cocreate solutions through playful thinking:** Invite team members to role-play, brainstorm with props, or draw out scenarios. Encourage creativity: "What's one playful way we could honor both structure and flexibility?" Emphasize collaboration: "How can we design this together?"
6. **Try out solutions:** Try different solutions and agree to check in and adjust as needed.
7. **Celebrate progress and reflection:** Acknowledge growth and teamwork. Reflect on progress and celebrate small milestones.

PAUSE AND REFLECT

- Considering the strategies that have been presented, what would you do to help Maria and Alex resolve their different perspectives?
- How could you use a play-based conflict resolution approach?

Let's explore how Iris approached the conflicting perspectives of Alex and Maria.

IRIS'S PLAY-BASED CONFLICT RESOLUTION APPROACH

Step 1: Observe First

Iris observed Maria and Alex's classroom. She could sense the tension between the two teachers as Maria was improvising a dramatic play activity while Alex looked frustrated that his small-group literacy activity was being disrupted. All the children wanted to be part of Maria's bakery in the block area. Maria seemed oblivious to the impact her actions were having on Alex's learning experience.

Step 2: Approach With Curiosity and Neutrality

At the end of the day, Iris entered Maria and Alex's classroom.

Iris: "I wanted to check in with both of you. I noticed some tension this morning during centers, and I'd like to hear more about what each of you were experiencing."

Step 3: Make Space for Each Voice

Maria: "I was following the children's excitement! They turned the blocks into a bakery. It felt like real learning was happening."

Alex: "I know they were engaged, but we had a literacy activity planned, and no one wanted to participate because everyone wanted to be part of your bakery. I had some specific skills that I planned to teach the children today."

Iris: "Thank you both for sharing. Let's take a playful pause. I know you both care deeply about our students and I appreciate your dedication. You share a passion for children's growth and development that focuses on school readiness. I would like to invite both of you to come with me to the break room to work on a design challenge." (They all go to the break room).

Iris: "On the table are some creative arts and building materials to use for your design challenge. You will each have fifteen minutes to build a model that shows what meaningful learning looks like in your classroom."

Maria eagerly started building a colorful open scene that included happy children, lots of art supplies and a pretend bakery in a rainbow of colors. Alex carefully constructed a neat classroom with labeled shelves, a visible schedule, books, and a teacher leading a small-group time.

Iris: "Time's up. You are each invited to share what you created."

Step 4: Identify the Core Issue Together

Maria: "This is my learning world. It is full of dramatic play, exploration, imagination, and choice. In the bakery children are learning by doing, practicing communication and teamwork. The rainbow of colors represents the joy and creativity children will have in this space."

Alex: "Mine is a more structured environment. Children know what to expect. The teacher is showing a concept clearly and guiding them with specific skills in mind. The children are focused. It's a calm and predictable environment where children feel safe and can meet learning goals."

Iris: "Both models are about care and connection. I'm hearing that Maria values spontaneous joy, and Alex values intentional focus. What if we imagined a way to bring those values together?"

Step 5: Cocreate Solutions Through Playful Thinking

Iris: "Let's use both of your models and see if we can add pieces to blend your styles during morning centers. Try adding something to your learning environment that connects to the other person's learning environment."

Maria added a clock to her play scene and Alex placed a tiny puppet in his scene.

Maria: "Routines help children feel safe. The clock represents adding more consistent structure without losing the joy."

Alex: "And structure can still be playful. Maybe I can use more play to teach the skills."

Iris: "That's the magic of play-based learning, it's not a trade-off, it's a bridge.

Maria: "I can see how important structure is to you. It is important to guide children to learn specific skills. What if we posted a play plan so children know what's coming, even when it's spontaneous?"

Alex: "And I could create small-group times that emerge from their play themes, like writing bakery menus."

Maria: "That's a great idea!"

Step 6: Try Out Solutions

Iris: "You are challenged to try out your ideas for the next two weeks. Then we will check in again and see what's working."

Step 7: Celebrate Progress and Reflection

Two weeks later . . .

Iris: "I've noticed your classroom feels more balanced, and the children are really thriving. How did the plan feel for you?"

Maria: "I feel like I am being creative and purposeful, although I have to keep reminding myself to be less spontaneous and follow our plan, because it's working."

Alex: "And I am seeing how play supports school readiness, not distracts from it."

Iris: "That is the power of blending your strengths!"

Outcome

Over time, Alex and Maria became more open to each other's perspectives. They started having open and frank discussions about their concerns and frustrations, and these honest discussions helped them develop a stronger bond. Iris observed their classroom and gave them feedback. She provided support and encouragement. Alex and Maria discovered that by blending their creative and structured approaches, they were able to experiment without sacrificing consistency. They were leveraging each person's strengths and noticing how different children responded to each approach. With time and patience, Alex and Maria were able to resolve their conflict and create a dynamic classroom where the children were thriving.

THE JOYFUL UPLIFT DIFFERENCE

Cultivating your team into an uplifting and joyful group will take time and effort. Some of the benefits of teams that work effectively are increased productivity and engaged employees. Playfulness is contagious. When leaders embrace it, teams feel energized and inspired. They are uplifted as they engage in simple acts of fun. Positive environments foster open communication, trust, and mutual respect. Team members are equipped to address conflicts constructively and navigate disagreements with empathy and respect. Playfulness can uplift staff, strengthen relationships, reduce stress, and enhance your workplace culture. By incorporating play into daily leadership, early childhood leaders can create an inspiring, supportive, and thriving environment for educators, children, and families.

INDIVIDUAL REFLECTION

1. Reflect on a time when playfulness helped lift your mood or ease a stressful situation at work. How did it impact your emotions and energy?
2. Think about ways you model playfulness as a leader. What else could you do?
3. Ponder on how playfulness could help your team manage stress and prevent burnout. What could your team do to reset and recharge during a challenging day?

BOOK GROUP OR DISCUSSION QUESTIONS

1. What are some actions leaders can take to become more playful versions of themselves? What slight changes could you make to create a more playful and joyful environment at work?
2. What challenges might arise as you become a more playful leader, and how could these challenges be addressed?

3. What are some team-building games or playful activities you could introduce to strengthen relationships and foster connections and collaboration?

UPLIFT IN ACTION

Select one or more of the following ideas to practice uplift in action.

- Play an upbeat song for a 1-minute dance party before meetings or at the end of the day.
- Plan a theme dress-up day such as Wacky Socks Day or Silly Accessory Day to bring laughter to the workplace.
- Create a random-acts-of-kindness bingo game with playful acts such as "Give someone an uplifting note," or "Make a colleague laugh," and celebrate those that complete a row on their bingo card.
- Give your team playful titles such as "chief optimism officer" or "director of joy."
- Leave bubble wrap in the breakroom for satisfying stress-relief popping.
- Provide markers and paper for a doodle wall where staff can contribute funny sketches or inspirational messages.
- Engage in playful team building activities such as a scavenger hunt or lip sync talent show.
- Invite team members to share playful memories from their childhood. Then challenge them to bring more playfulness into their classrooms.
- Implement play-based conflict resolution.

7

Hidden Blooms

Charmika "Mika" Hansen

Iris's Story

Iris gathered The Children's Garden employees for their monthly team meeting. She was planning to address some recent childcare center challenges while hoping to foster collaboration and unity. A sense of frustration had been brewing at The Children's Garden. Despite Iris's best efforts to uplift and motivate the team, certain employees seemed to resist every attempt at connection. These staff members included Lisa, a pessimistic veteran teacher; Jamal, a stressed-out employee juggling personal and professional struggles; Carla, who had been spreading gossip among colleagues; Alex, who was reluctant to participate with his coworkers; and Maria, who was struggling with issues in her

personal life. Their behaviors were not only affecting the team's morale but also impacted the overall culture of the center. Iris was not dissuaded. She liked to think of these employees as "hidden blooms" who just need a little extra help in order to thrive. Iris started the meeting: "Good morning, everyone. Thank you for being here today. I want to start by acknowledging the hard work you've all been putting in, especially during these busy weeks. Your dedication to the children and families we serve does not go unnoticed."

The team murmured their thanks, though the energy in the room was mixed. Lisa crossed her arms, her expression skeptical. Jamal slouched in his chair, rubbing his temples as though trying to shake off fatigue, and Carla leaned toward her neighbor, whispering something that earned a stifled giggle. Iris noticed that Alex was not even paying attention and was scrolling on his phone, while Maria stared off into space looking distraught.

Iris smiled and continued: "I'd like us to start with a quick check-in. Let's go around and share one thing you're proud of this week."

The team responded in turn, with varying levels of enthusiasm. Alex looked uncomfortable and avoided making eye contact with Iris in order to avoid speaking. Maria asked to be skipped when it was her turn to speak, and Iris gave her an understanding nod. When it was Lisa's turn, she sighed and said, "I guess I'm proud I survived another week. It's been chaotic with all the curriculum changes you asked for."

The team shifted uncomfortably. Carla nudged her neighbor and said something under her breath. Before Iris could respond to Lisa, Jamal cleared his throat and spoke next.

"I'm proud I managed to get through the week too, but honestly, it's been tough. Feels like there's always something more to do."

Iris nodded, taking in both comments. She sensed an opportunity to reframe the conversation. "Thank you, Lisa and Jamal. Your resilience is appreciated. I'd love to hear more about what's been particularly challenging so we can work together to address it." She paused to make eye contact with each of them, her tone warm and encouraging. Later, Iris noticed Carla whispering again.

Iris said, "Carla, I appreciate your enthusiasm, but I'd love for everyone to focus on our discussion right now. Let's save those side chats for later."

The meeting concluded with mixed results. Some employees left feeling energized by Iris's encouragement, while others remained hesitant or disengaged. Iris was still in the early stages as the new director of The Children's Garden and she knew that change can be slow. She was ready to take the next steps in addressing the team's challenges and planned to be consistent over time.

HIDDEN BLOOMS IN THE WORKPLACE

Imagine a beautiful garden, flourishing with vibrant flowers swaying in harmony with the gentle breeze. Roses blush in shades of red and pink, sunflowers stand tall and bright, and clusters of lavender, daisies, and marigolds add bursts of color while butterflies dance among the blooms. Each flower contributes to the beauty of the garden, but occasionally, there are hidden blooms—plants that have the potential to thrive but may be overshadowed, tangled, or in need of extra care. These hidden blooms symbolize the employees who may seem unresponsive to uplifting efforts or resistant to growth but, with the right attention, can flourish into valuable contributors to the team.

We've all encountered hidden blooms in some form. They may be the complainer who finds fault in every rule, the overburdened employee who struggles to see beyond their stress, or the distant colleague who keeps everyone at arm's length. Just as a gardener must find the right tools and techniques to nurture these plants, leaders must develop thoughtful strategies to help hidden blooms reach their full potential and create a thriving workplace culture (Goleman, 2006).

But before addressing hidden blooms, consider this: Haven't we all, at some point, been in this position? Can you think of a time when personal struggles, stress, or negativity clouded your ability to connect with others or embrace change? Recognizing this shared human experience can help you find the empathy and understanding needed to approach these employees with kindness and purpose (Fredrickson, 2004).

Hidden blooms have a profound effect on workplace culture. Like flowers that remain undernourished in a garden bed or become tangled with other stems, hidden blooms can deplete the energy and morale of a team. Even more concerning is the ripple effect; unchecked struggles can spread, much like weeds overtaking a garden, creating an atmosphere of discontent and disengagement. However, if you change your perspective, every hidden bloom presents an opportunity. Conflict and disengagement, when approached with curiosity and direct communication, can be the catalyst for profound growth and transformation (Tschannen-Moran, 2014). As leaders, we can nurture our workplace garden by tending to these hidden blooms with tools of honesty, empathy, acknowledgment, respect, and time—or HEART. As we explore the different types of hidden blooms we may encounter in the workplace, we will also explore the HEART framework more deeply and how it can be used to uplift everyone.

THE IMPACT OF TRAUMA ON EARLY EDUCATORS

Early childhood educators often face significant emotional burdens due to trauma. Many in this workforce carry their own adverse childhood experiences (ACE). According to Hubel et al. (2020), one study found that 73% of early care and education teachers had at least one ACE, and 22% reported four or more (Hubel et al., 2020). An ACE score refers to the number of adverse childhood experiences a person has encountered growing up, such as family instability, exposure to violence, or parental mental health challenges. The higher the score, the greater the potential impact on health and well-being (Hubel et al., 2020). Additionally, working daily with young children who experience trauma or chronic stress can lead to secondary traumatic stress (STS) in educators, which is a form of compassion fatigue. The toll of this exposure is profound. Educators frequently report anxiety, exhaustion, or emotional numbness that mirror the symptoms of trauma (Walker, 2019).

These trauma-related pressures also manifest as observable behaviors in the workplace, affecting interactions with colleagues and leaders (Luciw, 2023). Teachers suffering from unaddressed trauma or stress may become detached, mistrustful, or frustrated or feel isolated in professional relationships. Pollack (2025) explains that it is common for a chronically stressed teacher to withdraw socially and avoid staff gatherings or bids to collaborate. It is crucial to note that this is not rooted in defiance. These behaviors stem from a place of emotional exhaustion and a diminished capacity to connect. Similarly, such educators might show resistance to change when new policies or classroom initiatives are introduced. A teacher who has experienced past trauma or inconsistent support can become skeptical of new initiatives and crave the safety of familiar routines (Walker, 2019). Moreover, if previous efforts to work with the team or express themselves professionally were met with little support, these teachers may hesitate to trust leadership's decisions or to voice their needs. Over time, this combination of stress and unmet emotional needs contributes to educator burnout (Hubel et al., 2020). Supporting educators' mental well-being through trauma-informed leadership and empathetic support is, therefore, crucial for leaders looking to address challenges and uplift the hidden blooms within their programs.

IDENTIFYING THE HIDDEN BLOOMS

Weeds are flowers too, once you get to know them.

—Winnie The Pooh, A.A. Milne

Hidden blooms in the workplace can manifest in various ways. They are the individuals who seem immune to the culture of positivity and connection that leaders work so hard to cultivate. Hidden blooms may appear disengaged, skeptical, or even obstructive, often due to personal challenges, past experiences, or workplace dynamics that have eroded trust or motivation. However, they aren't inherently problematic or "bad" employees, but their behaviors can disrupt the workplace rhythm. When we take a step back, we might notice that the hidden blooms are often individuals who need deeper support and understanding to thrive.

We've all had a time in our lives when we felt resistant to change, negativity clouded our outlooks, or we struggled to accept help. Perhaps you were overwhelmed, disillusioned, or simply unable to see a way forward. Acknowledging these moments in our own lives fosters the empathy and patience required to work effectively with hidden blooms. It reminds us that pushback is often a signal, not an endpoint. It may signal a need for connection, clarity, or compassion.

Left unaddressed, hidden blooms can significantly impact workplace culture. Pessimism can dampen team morale; an overly stressed teacher can inadvertently spread anxiety to others; gossip can evoke shame and erode trust. When compounded, these attitudes and behaviors can lead to an emotionally taxing work environment for the whole team. Productivity often suffers, as the energy spent managing conflict or avoiding negativity detracts from focusing on goals. Over time, turnover rates may rise as high-performing employees seek healthier environments, leaving the team understaffed and overburdened (Walker, 2019). The ripple effect of negativity can undermine leadership, making it harder to foster engagement, innovation, and a shared sense of purpose within the organization. These behaviors can act like invasive weeds, taking up space and energy that could otherwise be directed toward growth.

Let's acknowledge that not every employee is a good fit for every workplace. There will be circumstances where the best decision is to remove the hidden bloom so that they may thrive in the right environment. However, I have a challenge for you to consider before making that decision. Instead of viewing these employees as an obstacle, can you reframe a hidden bloom as an opportunity? Conflict challenges us to dig deeper, ask questions, and find solutions. When approached with curiosity, understanding, and a focus on finding solutions, conflict can become fertile ground for innovation and connection (Schein, 2010).

HEART: A FRAMEWORK FOR ADDRESSING HIDDEN BLOOMS

The HEART framework is a simple yet powerful tool to approach hidden blooms with intention and care:

H̲onesty: Address the issue directly and transparently, avoiding ambiguity or sugar-coating.

E̲mpathy: Strive to understand the team member's perspective and underlying challenges.

A̲cknowledgment: Recognize the team member's feelings, concerns, or contributions.

R̲espect: Maintain a tone of professionalism and mutual regard, even in difficult conversations.

T̲ime: Allow for patience and persistence—change doesn't happen overnight.

By integrating HEART into daily interactions, leaders can create a safe space for hidden blooms to open and engage, which is imperative for a successful outcome (Bath, 2008). This approach not only addresses resistance but strengthens the fabric of the workplace, turning challenges into opportunities for collective growth.

PAUSE AND REFLECT

- Think of a time when you could have been identified as a hidden bloom. What kind of support did you need to thrive?
- Consider the HEART framework. If you were Iris, what would your next steps be after the team meeting?

HEART IN ACTION

Hidden blooms in the workplace are not monoliths. They come with unique challenges, personalities, and behaviors that require thoughtful approaches. Let's discover five common types of hidden blooms and observe how Iris tends to their needs in her center garden. We will explore the employee who is pessimistic, the employee who feels stressed-out, the employee who gossips and forms cliques, the employee who is distant, and the employee going through a hard time.

1. The Employee Who Is Pessimistic

The employee who is pessimistic often focuses on the negative, dismissing new ideas or expressing doubt about the team's goals. Their constant complaints can sap morale and hinder team progress. When addressing this team member, use honesty to point out the impact of their negativity, ask for their perspective on solutions, and acknowledge their concerns or past experiences. Focus on steering the conversation toward constructive action.

Remember Lisa and her negative comments during the team meeting? Iris is concerned about Lisa's negativity. Lisa is a seasoned toddler teacher known for her meticulous lesson plans. Unfortunately, she is equally known for her pessimism. Lisa often criticizes new ideas and policies, saying, "We've tried this before, and it never works," or "I don't see the point in changing what's already fine." Iris plans to schedule a one-on-one meeting with Lisa to dig deeper into her concerns and explore how Lisa's experience can inform team improvements. Iris plans to validate Lisa's concerns while reframing them as opportunities for growth. She will use the HEART approach.

Honesty

Iris: "Lisa, I've noticed that you've expressed concerns about new initiatives. I'd like to understand your perspective better."

Lisa: "It just feels like there's always new curriculum or best practice. It's frustrating to keep changing when I know what works for my classroom."

Empathy

Iris: "I can see that you're passionate about maintaining high standards and might be feeling unsure about these changes."

Lisa: "Exactly! I care about these kids and their learning. It's not that I don't want improvement, I just feel like our input as teachers isn't valued in these decisions."

Acknowledgment

Iris: "Your experience is invaluable, and I appreciate your dedication to what works."

Lisa: "I just wish we had more of a say. I've been here for years, and sometimes it feels like decisions are just handed down without considering what actually happens in the classroom."

Respect

Iris: "Let's explore how we can integrate your insights into this plan while addressing your concerns."

Lisa: "That would mean a lot. I just want to be heard and feel like I can contribute instead of just adapting to constant changes."

Time

Allow space for Lisa to adjust, inviting her to revisit the topic after the initial rollout.

Outcome

Lisa opens up about feeling excluded from decision-making processes. Iris invites Lisa to contribute to the center's upcoming curriculum review, leveraging her expertise while fostering collaboration. Lisa seems to thrive on this responsibility, and her negative comments have decreased each day.

2. The Employee Who Feels Stressed-Out

The employee who feels stressed-out is visibly overwhelmed, often rushing through tasks or expressing frustration. Their stress may stem from personal struggles, workload, or both. When addressing this team member, show empathy for their situation and offer resources or flexibility where possible. Respect their boundaries while encouraging open dialogue about their needs. Offer time to regroup, perhaps suggesting a mental health day or adjusting workloads temporarily.

Consider Jamal and his comments about feeling overwhelmed. Iris senses that he is stressed and takes the time to find out more. She discovers that Jamal, a new preschool teacher, is juggling multiple responsibilities, both at work and at home. He is a full-time student at the local community college while also taking on some of the responsibility of caring for his younger siblings. Recently, his interactions have been curt, and he's missed several deadlines, leaving his co-teacher to pick up the slack. Iris plans to offer Jamal flexible scheduling options and connect him with resources for time management and stress relief. She will be patient and show care while Jamal regains his footing. Iris will use the HEART approach.

Honesty

Iris: "Jamal, I've noticed you seem under a lot of stress lately. Is there something we can do to help?"

Jamal: "I just feel like I can't keep up. Between work, school, and helping my family, I'm stretched too thin."

Empathy

Iris: "Balancing so much can be overwhelming, and I want to support you."

Jamal: "I know I need to ask for help, but I don't want to let anyone down. It just feels like there's no time for anything."

Acknowledgment

Iris: "You've been a key contributor to this team, and we value your efforts."

Jamal: "I appreciate that, but I don't know how to lighten my load without dropping something important."

Respect

Iris: "Let's discuss a plan to balance your workload more effectively."

Jamal: "That would be really helpful. If I could just adjust my hours for a little while, I think I could manage things better."

Time

Schedule follow-ups to ensure that Jamal feels supported as he works through his challenges.

Outcome

Jamal admits he's overwhelmed by both work and personal responsibilities. Together, they develop a plan that includes lighter responsibilities for a few weeks and regular check-ins. Jamal is grateful for the flexibility to help him regroup. After a few weeks, Jamal is permanently working 30 hours, instead of 40, with the option of extra hours when needed. This has given him the chance to manage other aspects of his life. Jamal's mood has significantly improved!

3. The Employee Who Gossips and Forms Cliques

Gossip and cliques can quickly erode trust and morale within the workplace. A gossiping employee may unintentionally spread misinformation, creating divisions within the team and fueling an environment where cliques can thrive. These exclusive groups often isolate others, further damaging collaboration and inclusivity. When addressing gossip and cliques, be direct about their negative impact on team morale and trust. Acknowledge the influence these dynamics have within the workplace and redirect it toward fostering positive connections and inclusive behaviors. Encourage open communication and provide regular feedback and check-ins to address any underlying issues, helping to rebuild trust and strengthen team cohesion.

Think about Carla and her whispers during the team meeting. Iris is very concerned about her behavior. Carla is a recently hired assistant infant teacher who frequently shares unverified information about her colleagues, often framing it as concern: "Did you hear why Alex called in sick again? I bet it's more drama with him. He's always got something going on." Iris plans to reinforce the center's values during team meetings and privately discusses the impact of gossip with Carla. She will provide clear expectations while highlighting Carla's positive traits to redirect her energy. Iris will use the HEART approach.

Honesty

Iris: "Carla, I've noticed that some of your conversations about colleagues could lead to misunderstandings. Your comments can be perceived as hurtful or invasive."

Carla: "Oh, I didn't mean anything by it! I was just trying to keep people informed."

Empathy

Iris: "I understand that you may be coming from a place of concern, and I can tell you are interested in learning more about our team."

Carla: "Yeah, I guess I just like to know what's going on with everyone. It helps me feel connected."

Acknowledgment

Iris: "I recognize your intention to inform and communicate, but we need to ensure that we're respectful of everyone's privacy."

Carla: "I see what you mean. I wouldn't want anyone to feel uncomfortable because of something I said."

Respect

Iris: "Let's focus on fostering a positive, supportive environment. What do you think about helping me highlight staff members in our monthly newsletter?"

Carla: "That sounds like a great idea! I'd love to do that instead."

Time

Observe Carla over the next few months and reinforce the team's values during staff meetings to subtly guide future behavior.

Outcome

Carla didn't realize how negative her comments sounded and couldn't believe she had such an impact on the center staff. She apologizes and agrees to focus on positive contributions. Carla is excited about helping with the newsletter. She loves the opportunity to interview teachers and learn more about everyone on the team. In turn, the staff have really enjoyed the public acknowledgment of their hard work and personal accomplishments.

4. The Employee Who Is Distant

This individual keeps others at arm's length, avoiding interactions or feedback. They can be difficult to read, making it hard to build rapport. When addressing the employee who is distant, approach with patience and kindness, creating opportunities for connection without pressure. Consistently validate their unique strengths and contributions to the team. Allow time for them to acclimate, offering consistent support.

Recall Alex and his lack of interest in team meetings. Iris is concerned that he is distancing himself from the rest of the staff. Alex has been at The Children's Garden for about a year as an assistant preschool teacher. He has a good relationship with his classroom lead teacher; however, he rarely participates in team discussions and provides minimal responses to direct questions. The lead teacher he works with mentioned that Alex has wonderful ideas when it comes to the classroom, but it took him a while to start sharing. Other employees describe Alex as "hard to connect with." Iris is going to meet with Alex to learn more about how he feels working at The Children's Garden. She wants to emphasize how much she values his input and plans to come up with creative ways for Alex to share his ideas.

Honesty

Iris: "Alex, I've noticed you've been quiet during meetings. I'd really like to hear more of your thoughts."

Alex: "I just don't feel comfortable speaking up in big groups. I don't always know what to say."

Empathy

Iris: "I understand that group discussions might not be your preferred way to communicate."

Alex: "Yeah, I think better when I have time to process. I don't always come up with ideas on the spot."

Acknowledgment

Iris: "When you do share, your insights are always thoughtful and helpful"

Alex: "Thanks. I do care about the team. I just feel like my ideas get lost in the bigger conversations."

Respect

Iris: "Would you be open to sharing feedback in a way that's more comfortable? Let's brainstorm easy ways for you to contribute feedback. I don't want to miss out on your ideas!"

Alex: "Maybe I could write down my thoughts or talk with a smaller group instead of speaking in front of everyone."

Time

Build trust gradually by finding small opportunities to engage Alex during meetings and by checking in with one-on-one chats.

Outcome

Alex shares that he has always been shy, especially in front of large groups. He feels more comfortable discussing things with smaller groups. Alex also feels he can communicate best by writing things down. Iris has started adding partner discussions at staff meetings, as well as fun games that don't involve much discussion (BINGO, for example). She has also found great success in encouraging staff members to plan and lead their own team-building activities! Iris also added a suggestion box to the break room and reiterated to Alex that he can always come talk with her anytime. Alex has participated more in team meetings, has shared written ideas, and has provided invaluable feedback!

5. The Employee Going Through a Hard Time

Sometimes conflict stems from personal hardships, like grief, financial struggles, or health challenges. When addressing the employee going through a hard time, lead with empathy, recognizing the depth of their personal challenges. Offer flexibility, whether through adjusted duties or time off. When appropriate, offer resources that could be helpful for their situation. Respect their privacy while ensuring they know support is available.

Remember Maria and her melancholy behavior during the team meeting? Iris knows that she is currently going through a hard time. Maria is an excellent preschool lead teacher and has worked at The Children's Garden for over 10 years. Usually warm and friendly, Maria has recently been withdrawn and frequently late to work. A colleague mentioned that she recently separated from her husband and is struggling to adjust. In this case, Iris is truly concerned about Maria's well-being and wants to offer support however she can. Iris will sit down with Maria and approach with HEART.

Honesty

Iris: "Maria, I've noticed you seem to be having a tough time lately. I'm here if you want to talk or need support."

Maria: "I've just been feeling overwhelmed. It's hard to focus at work when everything in my personal life feels like a mess."

Empathy

Iris: "It's okay to feel however you are feeling, and I want to make sure you have what you need to be supported."

Maria: "I appreciate that. I don't want my personal struggles to affect my work, but it's been hard to keep everything together."

Acknowledgment

Iris: "You are an amazing teacher and an invaluable part of this team. I really want to be there for you during this time."

Maria: "That means a lot. I don't want to let anyone down, but I could use a little breathing room."

Respect

Iris: "Let's discuss any adjustments we can make to help you navigate this period."

Maria: "Maybe just a couple of days off or some flexibility in my schedule would help me get back on track."

Time

Provide flexibility, like adjusted schedules or reduced responsibilities, as Maria works through her challenges.

Outcome

Maria cries and expresses how much Iris's concern means to her. She admits that she is struggling with the separation from her husband, but she knows it's the best decision. Together, Maria and Iris come up with a plan: Maria will take two mental health days, giving her a 4-day weekend to decompress. Iris helps Maria find a therapist that is covered by the center employee health plan. Maria's situation is hard and will take time to navigate, but Iris notices improvement week by week. Maria has learned to ask for help and take time off when she needs a break.

THE CHILDREN'S GARDEN

Over time, Iris noticed improvements in team dynamics at The Children's Garden. Lisa became a proactive contributor, Jamal appeared less stressed and more engaged, Carla channeled her energy into building team morale, Alex became more vocal, and Maria's healing journey was slow but steady. Iris reflected on her leadership style and started adapting meetings to meet the needs of the employees. She introduced fun team-building experiences to improve cohesion and morale and found great success with allowing team members to plan and lead their own fun activities. Challenges remain, but The Children's Garden was beginning to thrive under Iris's consistent, thoughtful, and caring leadership.

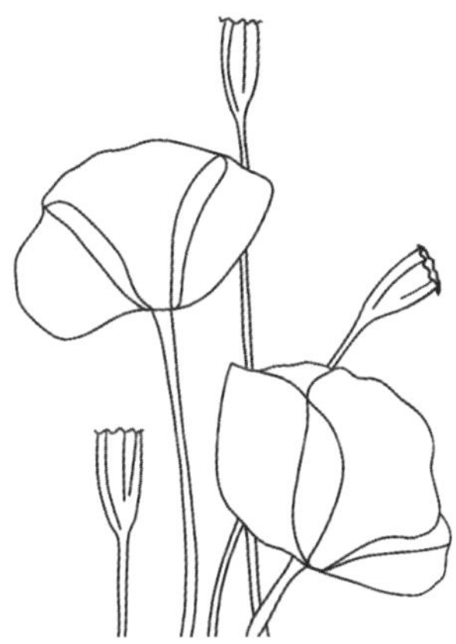

THE JOYFUL UPLIFT DIFFERENCE

Addressing hidden blooms in the workplace requires leaders to step into the role of caring gardeners, tending to relationships with patience, curiosity, and intentionality. Conflict and resistance, while challenging, present an opportunity for growth for both individuals and the team. By embracing direct communication with HEART (honesty, empathy, acknowledgment, respect, and time), leaders can navigate difficult dynamics and create a culture where even the most nutrient-depleted hidden blooms can thrive. Through tailored approaches, continuous reflection, and a commitment to fostering connection, leaders can transform hidden blooms into thriving blossoms, paving the way for a more joyful and productive workplace.

INDIVIDUAL REFLECTION

1. Think of a time when you were resistant to change or connection. What factors contributed to your resistance?

2. How have you responded to hidden blooms in your workplace? What worked, and what could you improve?

3. Which strategies presented in this chapter resonate most with you, and how might you apply them to your team?

BOOK GROUP OR DISCUSSION QUESTIONS

1. Reflect on the HEART framework. Which component do you feel most confident using, and which could you strengthen?

   Honesty: Address the issue directly and transparently, avoiding ambiguity or sugar-coating.

   Empathy: Strive to understand the team member's perspective and underlying challenges.

   Acknowledgment: Recognize the team member's feelings, concerns, or contributions.

   Respect: Maintain a tone of professionalism and mutual regard, even in difficult conversations.

   Time: Allow for patience and persistence. Change doesn't happen overnight.

2. How do different types of hidden blooms (e.g., pessimism, stress, gossip) require distinct approaches? Share examples.

3. What are the potential long-term benefits of addressing hidden blooms effectively for team morale and workplace culture?

UPLIFT IN ACTION

Select one or more of the following ways to uplift the "hidden blooms" in your workplace:

- Reach out privately to a colleague who seems withdrawn and offer a listening ear.
- Acknowledge a team member's specific strength or contribution that may go unnoticed, especially if they've been struggling or appear discouraged.
- Reframe a challenging behavior with empathy. Pause and consider, "What support might this person need right now?"
- Practice transparency and honesty with a colleague about a recent change or policy. Invite their perspective and listen without judgment.
- Offer flexibility or resources to a colleague going through a tough time.
- Commit to addressing gossip or negative talk directly and redirecting the energy toward collaboration and positive recognition.

8

Joyfully Uplifting Families

Charmika "Mika" Hansen and Danielle Pertile

MS. DAWN'S SUNSHINE

At the childcare center where I (Danielle) worked before becoming a trainer, our front desk administrator was Ms. Dawn. She had a larger-than-life personality and a boisterous laugh that drew you in immediately. Ms. Dawn greeted every child and family by name and remembered details about their favorite activities outside school.

When I had my son and began bringing him to our infant room, I loved stopping by Ms. Dawn's desk to say goodnight before leaving. She would make silly faces at him while he sat in his forward-facing infant carrier, and I'd watch his little cheeks rise in a big, joyful smile.

Sadly, Ms. Dawn passed away a few years after I left the center. When my family and I attended her memorial service, it was incredible and heartwarming to see how many families showed up to honor her, each with heartfelt stories. Though Ms. Dawn didn't typically work in the classrooms, her warmth and care left a lasting impression on every family she met. The sunshine she brought to the center uplifted everyone who walked through the door.

THE FAMILY IMPACT

Researchers consistently highlight that intentional family engagement significantly enhances children's academic achievement, emotional well-being, and social skills. Families are a child's first and most influential educators. When schools and families work together intentionally, the benefits multiply.

Children benefit tremendously when they see their families and educators working together. Consistent communication helps them feel safe and supported, reducing anxiety and boosting self-confidence. Emotionally, children thrive when they sense harmony and mutual respect among the adults in their lives, fostering strong self-esteem and healthy development (Koralek et al., 2019; Lewis et al., 2023). Socially, engaged families model empathy, cooperation, and positive interactions, laying a strong foundation for children's relationships with others.

Family engagement also positively impacts educators. Teachers who build strong, collaborative relationships with families report higher confidence in their teaching skills and more positive relationships with the children in their classrooms (Sheridan & Kim, 2015). These partnerships foster open communication, making it easier to address concerns early and effectively. Engaged families often become active allies and advocates, reinforcing shared values and strengthening the overall school community.

Ultimately, prioritizing family engagement enriches the entire educational ecosystem. Schools become more than academic institutions; they evolve into inclusive, supportive communities where children, families, and educators experience connection, growth, and belonging (Baker et al., 2016). When families are intentionally uplifted, their engagement contributes powerfully to their children's resilience, joy, and long-term success.

Iris's Story

When Iris became director of The Children's Garden, she noticed a troubling pattern: Families would drop off their children and leave quickly, rarely interacting with staff. It wasn't out of rudeness. Instead, there was a lack of connection.

Take Sophia, for example. Every morning, she quietly entered with her 3-year-old son, Mateo, eyes down, walking briskly to the classroom. After a quick hug, she would leave without a word. Iris understood that families had busy mornings, but she also believed that building relationships with every caregiver was essential.

One morning, Iris paused at the entrance and greeted Sophia and Mateo with a warm smile, asking how Sophia was doing. Surprised but appreciative, Sophia shared her struggles with Mateo's sleep schedule. Iris, having faced similar challenges, recommended a bedtime routine that had worked well for her own son when he was little. That short but sincere conversation sparked something in Iris, and she was determined to find even more ways to engage the wonderful families at The Children's Garden.

CULTIVATING THE FAMILY GARDEN

Just as early childhood leaders nurture their team with care and attention, we must also approach families with the same intentional care. If teachers are the radiant flower garden of a center, families are the robust herb garden: providing unique flavors, fragrances, and contributions. Every family member of a child enrolled in your center brings their own strengths, cultures, and experiences. Recognizing and celebrating these differences fosters a deeper sense of community and belonging. Like an experienced gardener who knows that oregano prefers sun while parsley thrives in cool shade, educators must adapt to each family's needs and preferences to help them flourish.

Some families, like the herbs thyme and mint, flourish naturally. Others, like basil or rosemary, need more time and attention before revealing their richness. These are the families who are quiet, distant, or hesitant. Like herbs growing in challenging conditions, these families may be overshadowed by past negative experiences or are navigating personal hardships. However, we can gently nurture these relationships, adjusting our approach to ensure that each family receives the precise care they require to thrive.

Over time, caring attention and individualized support can add unexpected richness to the program community. As educators and leaders, we are gardeners working to plant seeds of trust, watering relationships with empathy, validation, and support. When families feel authentically valued and uplifted, their engagement grows. Relationships deepen, trust is built, and the ripple effects strengthen the entire community (Baker et al., 2016; Friedman & Mwenelupembe, 2020). Together, we can create a nurturing space where children, families, and educators grow stronger, healthier, and more connected.

FIVE STRATEGIES FOR JOYFULLY UPLIFTING FAMILIES

Tending to a vibrant herb garden requires thoughtful, consistent care and we should apply this same mindset to nurturing family–school partnerships. Joyce Epstein's (2009) model of family engagement outlines six key types of involvement that support student success: parenting, communicating, volunteering, learning at home, decision making, and collaborating with the community. This model emphasizes the shared responsibility between schools, families, and communities in promoting student learning and development. Epstein's framework, paired with the spirit of uplifting others, can support schools in creating a welcoming environment where all families feel valued and empowered to participate.

When programs uplift families with authenticity and intention, connections are built and families engage more joyfully in their children's education. The following five "herbal" strategies align with Epstein's model of family engagement principles and offer practical ways to build inclusive, trusting, and joyful partnerships with families:

1. Communicate and build connections: rosemary
2. Celebrate family strengths and cultural heritage: basil
3. Cultivate fresh engagement: mint
4. Build a cohesive community: thyme
5. Navigate family challenges with care: chamomile

See Table 8.1 (page 112) for herbal strategies and Joyce Epstein's Model of Family Engagement Alignment chart. These strategies serve as a symbolic guide for cultivating strong, sustainable family partnerships.

1. Rosemary: Communicate and Build Connections

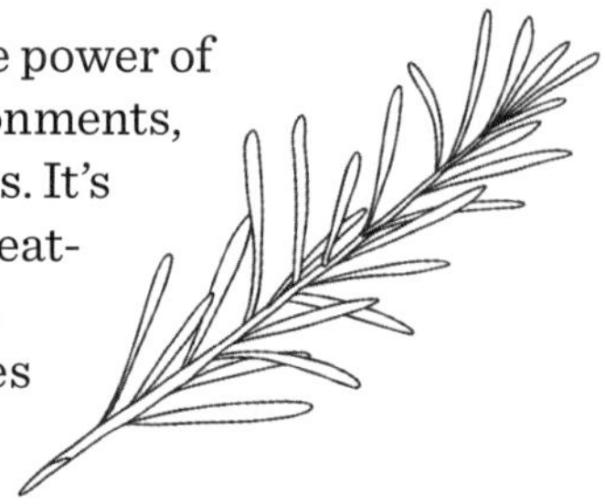

Rosemary, a symbol of remembrance and loyalty, reflects the power of meaningful, lasting communication. In early learning environments, meaningful communication is more than exchanging updates. It's about building trust, fostering mutual understanding, and creating spaces where families feel genuinely connected and seen. When communication is intentional and heartfelt, it creates a supportive environment where children and families thrive.

Setting the Tone for Connection

Program leaders set the tone by prioritizing family partnerships and equipping staff with the tools they need. This includes professional development on communication skills and family engagement strategies, while also teaching the benefits of successful family engagement. Teachers may feel more receptive when they understand that partnering with families can lead to deeper understanding of their students and improved student outcomes (Vance, 2024). Professional development should also include a strong emphasis on cultural responsiveness, which is defined as the ability to recognize, understand, and honor the diverse cultural backgrounds of children and families

(Choi & Bigelow, 2024). When teachers feel supported and prepared, they're more confident and consistent in connecting with families.

Personalized Welcomes

A warm, personalized welcome sets a positive tone. Greeting families by name and showing genuine interest in their well-being sends a clear message: *You matter here.* Consider posting short welcome notes or sending personalized messages to celebrate a child's milestone or thank a family for their support. You can also incorporate greetings in families' home languages. While fluency isn't necessary, learning to say simple words like "hello" or "good morning" shows thoughtfulness and intention.

Joyful, Strengths-Based Updates

Frequent, joyful updates help families feel connected and appreciated. A simple photo and story such as "CeCe faced her fear and slid down the slide today! We're so proud of her bravery" can spark smiles and reinforce shared joy. These messages help families feel seen not just as caregivers, but as partners in their child's journey. Focusing on their child's strengths (what they are doing well) allows families to notice and encourage those strengths at home, too (Knoche & Witte, 2016; Waters et al., 2018).

Listening With Intention

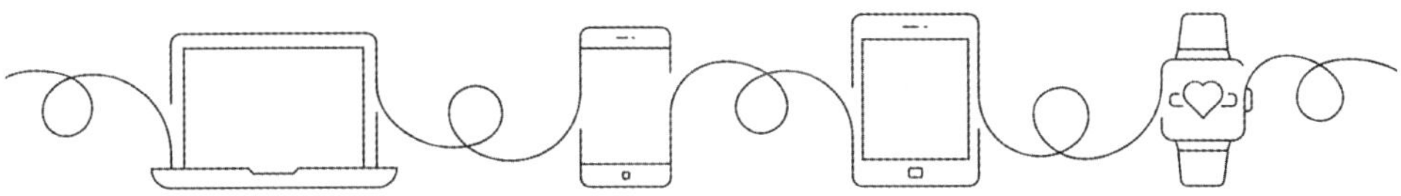

Active listening means creating space for families to share and be heard. Use accessible channels such as texts, calls, apps, notes, or emails to meet families where they feel most comfortable. Show that you're listening by responding with care, affirming their perspectives, and inviting input. Every interaction is an opportunity to strengthen trust and build community.

Supporting Teacher Confidence

Some teachers enter the profession passionate about children but feeling uncertain about family engagement. Concerns about saying the wrong thing or navigating cultural differences are common and valid. The first step toward building confidence is self-reflection that examines beliefs, communication habits, and assumptions.

Mentorship is another powerful tool. By connecting with trusted colleagues, such as a more experienced teacher, newer teachers can gain insight and guidance as they build their confidence. Most importantly, teachers should be encouraged to start with small, intentional actions, such as greeting families warmly or sharing a child's success, to lay the foundation for deeper relationships.

Gratitude as a Daily Practice

Gratitude deepens trust and joy. A simple, sincere thank you such as "Thanks for the extra snacks!" or "We appreciate your morning smiles!" can help families feel valued. Make gratitude visible through thank-you notes, weekly appreciation messages, or designated spaces like a gratitude tree or wall of thanks. Public recognition, such as social media shout-outs or "Fantastic Family Friday" features, can also uplift families; just be sure to honor privacy preferences. Whether quiet or public, consistent appreciation tells families they are an essential part of the program.

PAUSE AND REFLECT

- What will you do to build your staff's confidence to uplift families?
- Think of a time when meaningful communication strengthened your relationship with a family. How can you recreate or build on that experience with other families?

2. Basil: Celebrate Family Strengths and Cultural Heritage

Basil, often called the "herb of love," is known for its nurturing and revitalizing qualities. In our metaphorical family garden, basil represents the importance of nourishing relationships by honoring families as a child's first and most influential teachers. Just as herbs bring unique flavors to a garden, families enrich early learning communities with diverse values, traditions, and experiences.

When educators intentionally celebrate what families bring, they affirm that every caregiver belongs and their contributions matter. This not only strengthens trust and connection but also helps children see their culture reflected in the classroom, enhancing their sense of identity and belonging (Fox & Swett, 2017).

Getting to Know Families

To honor families authentically, we first need to understand who they are. A simple "Getting to Know Your Family" questionnaire at the beginning of the year or when a new family enrolls can help open the door (see Appendix A). Keep it brief, welcoming, and culturally sensitive. Sample prompts might include

- What makes your family unique?
- What holidays or traditions do you celebrate?

- How do you comfort your child when they're upset?
- Is there anything you'd like us to know about your child's culture, language, or family story?

Information can also be gathered informally through quick check-ins, conversations during drop-off and pick-up, or simple polls. The key is to listen and reflect what you learn. When families see their language, customs, or values incorporated, such as a lullaby in their home language or a traditional recipe featured, they feel truly seen.

Celebrating Family Milestones

Families experience many life events outside school: births, birthdays, new jobs, graduations, or major changes like a move or deployment. Recognizing these moments honors each family's broader journey. Consider keeping a (voluntary) milestone calendar and acknowledge events with a small gesture such as a card, classroom mention, or group activity.

Examples:

- "Liam became a big brother, congratulations to his whole family!"
- "Let's make a card for Jordan's mom. She just graduated nursing school!"
- "Xavier's family moved. Let's create artwork to help decorate his new room."

These recognitions, whether big or small, show families that you care about them as whole people, not just in their role as parents. They also teach children to celebrate others with empathy and kindness.

Family Culture Days and Story Sharing

Hosting periodic family culture days invites families to share their heritage in meaningful, accessible ways. They might bring in a favorite recipe, teach a traditional dance, share a family song, or tell a cherished story. Some families may prefer to send items or notes from home rather than present in person; as always, flexibility is key. These events build pride, strengthen cultural identity, and expose children to the rich diversity of their peers. Watching a classmate's family traditions come to life in the classroom fosters both connection and curiosity.

Family Spotlights

Dedicate a space in your program such as a "Family Spotlight" board or newsletter section to celebrate different families on a rotating basis. This could include photos, favorite foods or books, family traditions, or fun facts. Be intentional about representation: highlight single-parent households, LGBTQ+ families, multigenerational caregivers, military and foster families, and families who speak languages other than English. The goal is for every child to see their own family celebrated and to recognize the value in others' unique stories. A family spotlight reminds everyone that every kind of family belongs and contributes something meaningful to the community.

PAUSE AND REFLECT

- What ways do you get to know the families in your program? How can you learn more?
- What family stories, strengths, or traditions could you highlight more intentionally in your program?

3. Mint: Cultivate Fresh Engagement

Mint is versatile and brings a burst of invigorating energy to the garden. In the same way, refreshing our approach to family engagement can breathe new life into early learning programs. This strategy encourages us to go beyond the usual invitations and cultivate new, flexible ways for families to connect, contribute, and feel part of the learning community. When participation is fun, accessible, and meaningful, families are more likely to engage and stay engaged.

Valuing Families' Skills, Time, and Talents

Every family brings unique strengths. One parent might be an artist, another a gardener. A grandparent might be a storyteller or a handy carpenter. The key to making engagement accessible is offering options that make it easy for families to contribute in ways that suit their interests, availability, and comfort levels. Consider creating a "Menu of Participation," which is a simple form families complete at the start of the year and revisit throughout the year. This menu can include ideas such as

- reading a story (in any language)
- sharing a favorite family recipe
- leading a music or movement activity
- sharing a cultural item or holiday tradition
- recording a short video or voice note for the class
- helping prepare activity materials from home such as cutting, laminating, stapling, and so forth
- supporting educators in hanging artwork or decorating bulletin boards, doors, or classroom walls
- assisting with a class project, garden, or event
- connecting with local businesses to donate supplies

Be sure to include a blank space for families to write in their own suggestions as well, and offer at-home options for families who can't attend in person. By valuing families' time and talents, you reinforce that your program is cocreated *with* them, not just *for* them.

Creative Gatherings and Events

Family events are another "minty fresh" way to build relationships and a sense of community (see Appendix B on the Brookes Download Hub for a reproducible version of Fun Family Engagement Ideas). Prioritize offering different types of events, on different days and times, to increase accessibility, for example,

- a weekday picnic on the playground
- a Friday evening "Pizza and Game Night"
- a Saturday morning field trip to a local park or pumpkin patch

While not every family can attend every event, offering a mix increases the chance that everyone can participate in something. Even a small group can create lasting memories. Additionally, you can share photos or event highlights afterward, so others feel included. These gatherings strengthen family-to-family connections and help caregivers see the center as a place where they, too, belong.

Inclusive Celebrations: Rethinking Holidays

Traditional holiday events, though well-intentioned, can sometimes feel exclusive or awkward for some families. A more inclusive approach is to reframe how and what you celebrate. For instance,

- Instead of "Mother's Day Tea" or "Father's Day Breakfast," host a "Family Day" or "Special Person Celebration" where every child can invite someone meaningful.
- Rather than focusing on one cultural tradition (like Christmas), try a "Winter Celebrations Around the World" event that welcomes a variety of traditions, holidays, and customs.

This flexible approach welcomes all family types and honors the richness of diverse experiences. It reduces pressure and fosters shared joy and learning across your school community. Children also benefit when they see their families and others' traditions reflected because we can model respect, curiosity, and connection.

PAUSE AND REFLECT

- What creative, flexible participation options could you include in your own Menu of Participation?
- What has been one of your favorite family engagement activities or events? What could you do to make it even more inclusive for families in your program?

4. Thyme: Build a Cohesive Community

Thyme has long symbolized courage and connection, which are qualities at the heart of strong communities. In our family garden, thyme reminds us that families thrive when rooted in meaningful relationships, both within the program and in the broader world. We often hear the old proverb, "It takes a village to raise a child," but in our fast-paced and often disconnected society, many families struggle to find that village. Your childcare center can help fill that gap by fostering connections among families and creating a supportive, lasting network of care. Here are some ways to grow that kind of community.

Buddy Families: Mentorship Builds Belonging

Many of us remember school "buddy" systems where older students helped younger ones adjust. The same idea can be used to build bridges among families. Invite returning families (who've been at your center for at least a year) to serve as buddy families for newcomers. Participation is optional but meaningful; buddies might exchange contact info, offer a warm welcome, or pair up for events and classroom projects. These low-pressure relationships can blossom into trust and belonging, easing the transition for new families and deepening the sense of community across your program.

Inviting Families Into Program Decisions

Community grows when people feel heard. One powerful way to build that trust is by involving families in programming decisions. This can range from a formal parent advisory board to informal methods like surveys, suggestion jars, or

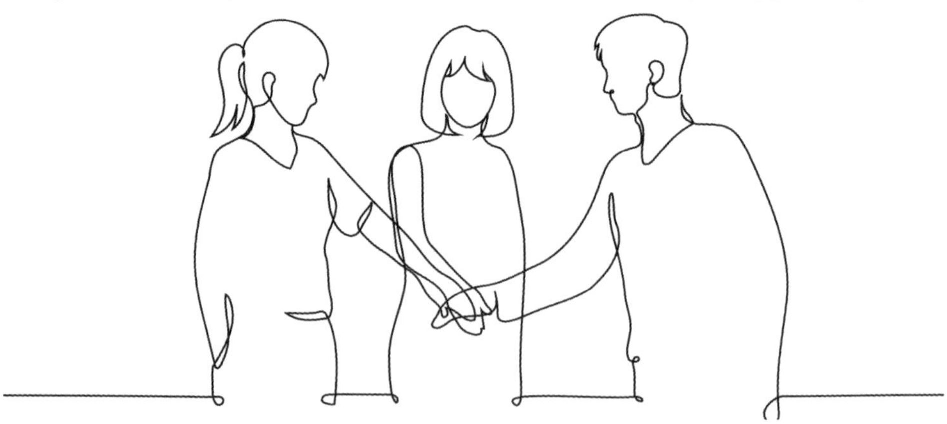

occasional input forms. Whether families help choose a field trip, revise a snack policy, or recommend a local cause to support, the message is clear: Their voice matters. Consider hosting quarterly family forums (offer in person and virtual options) to share updates, gather input, and cocreate solutions. When families see their feedback acknowledged and acted upon—or clearly explained when it isn't feasible—they develop a stronger sense of ownership and partnership.

Designing Welcoming Spaces for Families

As discussed in Chapter 5, physical environments shape emotional experiences. Your center's layout can communicate whether families feel like guests or like they belong. Here are four ways to create family-friendly community spaces:

- ***Family Lobby and Activity Area***

  Some families rush through drop-off and pick-up, while others need a slower transition, especially those with younger children or who are new to your center. A cozy, inviting area with simple materials like crayons, wooden blocks, or books allows for quiet connection before and after class. It also gives new families something to engage with during tours or enrollment visits, easing first impressions.

- ***Nursing Room***

  For parents who breastfeed, having a quiet, private space to nurse honors the parent–child bond and supports a gentle start to the day. If you don't have a dedicated room, consider flexible solutions, such as a sign for an office door or a curtained alcove with a comfy chair and soft lighting. A little privacy goes a long way in making families feel respected and cared for.

- ***Coffee and Tea Station***

  A small beverage station stocked with coffee, tea, and water invites families to pause and connect. This simple offering helps ease the emotional transition at drop-off and encourages friendly interactions among parents. If budget is a concern, a "tip jar" or local sponsorships can help sustain it. Bonus idea: Place the station near a classroom monitor so parents can sip while watching their child settle in.

- ***Food Pantry and Mutual Aid Resources***

  Basic needs support is a powerful way to care for the whole community. One center in northern Nevada, led by director Antonia Ward, created a food pantry through local partnerships and grants. All enrolled families, staff, and even community members can access the pantry without stigma or strings. While not every center can maintain a full pantry, you might start small:

  - Partner with local food banks or service groups.
  - Collect donations of gently used children's clothing, coats, or shoes.

- Accept supplies like diapers and wipes from businesses or families.

As we acknowledged in Chapter 5, offering these resources can seem unattainable, expensive, or time-consuming. However, this is another opportunity to invite families to contribute, donate, and volunteer in ways that work for them. Keep in mind that even modest efforts send a clear message: This is a community that cares for one another.

PAUSE AND REFLECT

- What's one concrete action you can take to help build a "village" of support among families in your care?
- How and where can you create a warm, welcoming family space within your program?

5. Chamomile: Navigate Family Challenges With Care

Chamomile is known for its soothing and restorative qualities. In our garden of strategies, chamomile represents the calm, compassionate support we offer to families during challenging times. Even in a joyful, connected school community, families will encounter difficulties, whether it's a tough conversation, a family crisis or trauma, or a misunderstanding between parent and teacher. This strategy is about meeting those moments with empathy, patience, and a solution-focused mindset. By doing so, we protect and strengthen the relationships we've built, even when times are hard.

Approaching Hard Conversations With Empathy

Discussing concerns, such as a child's challenging behavior, requires thoughtfulness. Choose a quiet, private space and allow enough time for open, unhurried dialogue. Begin by highlighting the child's strengths to set a positive tone, and then clearly and kindly share your concerns (Kottler & Kottler, 2015). Always invite the family's perspective. Listen deeply and approach the conversation as a partnership with the shared goal of helping their child thrive. A respectful, collaborative tone builds trust and makes problem-solving more effective.

Supporting Families Through Personal Crises

Families may face hardships like illness, divorce, job loss, or trauma. In these moments, your role as a consistent, caring presence is critical. You might

- adjust classroom expectations or schedules temporarily
- offer referrals to community resources
- maintain regular check-ins
- simply be available to listen

Children under stress may act out or regress. Respond with extra patience, structure, and reassurance. Respect families' privacy, but make sure they know your program is a safe, supportive space for both parent and child (Bath, 2008). Compassion during crisis builds bonds that last long beyond the hard season.

Rebuilding After Conflict

Even in the best partnerships, misunderstandings and conflicts will happen. If tensions arise, it's important to be proactive (Dwyer & Buckle, 2009). Once emotions settle, reach out and invite a conversation. Whether it's a hurt feeling or a policy concern, take time to listen without defensiveness. Apologize if needed, clarify misunderstandings, and express your desire to move forward positively. In-person or phone conversations often resolve things more effectively than email. Before wrapping up, agree on one small step to improve the relationship moving forward. Taking initiative to repair trust shows that you care about the family relationship, especially when it's hard.

Creating Peer Support Groups

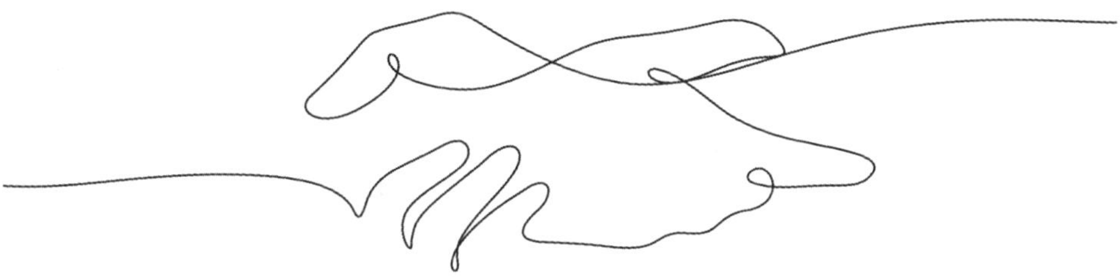

Families often benefit from connecting with others who share similar experiences. Consider facilitating or encouraging support groups that can meet at your center or in community spaces like libraries or parks. Groups might focus on

- divorce or separation
- military deployment
- grief or illness
- addiction or incarceration
- parenting neurodivergent children
- potty training support
- positive guidance and discipline
- kindergarten transition

You can help by offering a meeting space, making introductions (with permission), or inviting a guest speaker like a child therapist. Sometimes, all that's needed is coffee, time, and a safe space for connection.

The Heart of the Chamomile Strategy

Chamomile care means families feel seen, heard, and supported, especially when things aren't going smoothly. This kind of care builds lasting trust and models for children how compassion works within a community. When families feel heard through their hardest moments, they often become your strongest allies and are eager to support others in return. The strength of your school community lies not in the absence of challenges but in how you respond to them. Lead with grace, empathy, and genuine partnership.

PAUSE AND REFLECT

- What support group topics would be most meaningful for families in your program?
- How can your center respond with care and flexibility when a family is in crisis?

Iris's Approach

Inspired by her interaction with Sophia and Mateo, Iris began spending the first 30 minutes of each morning at the front desk, intentionally greeting families. Over time, she noticed a shift: Parents began walking in with smiles, chatting

Table 8.1.

Herbal Strategies and Joyce Epstein's Model of Family Engagement Alignment Chart

Herbal strategy	Uplifting focus	Epstein pillar alignment
Communicate & build connections: rosemary	Prioritize meaningful and consistent interactions while fostering bidirectional communication and collaboration	Communicating, decision making
Celebrate family strengths & cultural heritage: basil	Honor every child and their family's unique story and traditions Encourage & welcome different kinds of contributions from families	Communicating, parenting, & volunteering
Cultivate fresh engagement: mint	Offer flexible, fun, and original opportunities for center, classroom, and home engagement tailored to the needs and availability of families	Communicating, volunteering, learning at home
Build a cohesive community: thyme	Foster genuine connections among families, provide a space for community, and build a network of support	Parenting, communicating, collaborating with the community
Navigate family challenges with care: chamomile	Offer calm and compassionate support, as well as community resources to families Listen, validate, & approach conflict with curiosity	Communicating, decision making

about their lives and their children. The center began to feel warmer, more connected.

As Iris and her team brought each strategy to life, The Children's Garden transformed into a true second home for families. Communication between teachers and parents became more open and positive. The lobby bloomed with family photos, thank-you notes, and drawings.

Monthly events like pajama and pancake mornings and park meetups built friendships among families who'd never spoken before. A cozy coffee station near the entrance sparked morning conversations and check-ins. The buddy family program connected new and veteran families, with relationships that extended beyond school walls. Parents contributed to classroom projects, shared cultural traditions, and even led story time. As trust deepened, joy grew. What once were quiet, hurried drop-offs became warm, collaborative mornings filled with connection.

THE JOYFUL UPLIFT DIFFERENCE

Just like a flourishing garden needs ongoing care, meaningful relationships with families require attention, empathy, and sincere communication. When families feel truly uplifted and valued, they contribute more deeply, creating a ripple effect of connection and trust.

By tending your garden with intention, you help cultivate a vibrant community where children, families, and educators grow and thrive together.

INDIVIDUAL REFLECTION

1. Think of a family that is currently disconnected or resistant. How can you apply the five strategies to nurture connection?
    a. Rosemary: Communicate and build connections
    b. Basil: Celebrate family strengths and cultural heritage
    c. Mint: Cultivate fresh engagement
    d. Thyme: Build a cohesive community
    e. Chamomile: Navigate family challenges with care
2. Reflect on a time when family engagement transformed your classroom or center. What led to this positive change?
3. What creates feelings of gratitude for you when thinking about the families in your program?

BOOK GROUP OR DISCUSSION QUESTIONS

1. How can applying the five strategies deepen trust with families in your program?

2. Share successful examples of how your program has joyfully uplifted families. What made these efforts effective?
3. Discuss the long-term impacts of intentionally uplifting family engagement. How does this benefit children, families, and staff?

UPLIFT IN ACTION

Select one or more actions to uplift families today:

- Spend time in the lobby of your program during pick-up or drop-off and greet families personally.
- Write down at least five different ways families can become active participants.
- Choose a few families each week to send a quick email to say thank you or to recognize something special (whether it's a creative lunch, a positive attitude at drop-off, or a donation to the classroom).
- Ask families to submit their favorite parenting or family tip (e.g., "bedtime story rituals," "how we calm down after a tough day," or "favorite weekend activity"). Display these tips on a family board or include them in a newsletter.
- Invite families to share a favorite recipe (with a story or photo if they wish). Combine the recipes into a printed or digital "Family Recipe Book" to share with everyone.
- Set up an area in your center where families can access information on community resources (flyers, brochures, websites, business cards, coupons, etc.). Consider providing internet, computer, or printer access.

9

Uplifting and Managing Change with Confidence

Geraldine "Gigi" Wynn

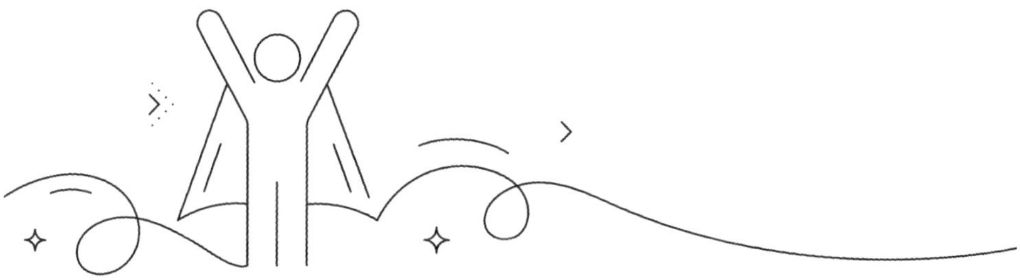

Managing change with confidence is something that I have learned, and I continue to acquire new skills throughout my career in the early childhood field. The word "manage" has several different definitions from different sources, but the most common one derives from the Merriam-Webster dictionary. It states that the word "manage" means to handle or direct with a degree of skill such as to exercise executive administrative and supervisory direction of a business (Merriam-Webster, 2025). I noticed when reading this definition that it does not mention the confidence needed when managing. Confidence is a skill one needs to intentionally develop. Confidence is not a potion, ready-mixed and to a set recipe: It's a palette (The Company Agency Leadership Council et al., 2009). It does not come in one size fits all. "The word confidence is defined as the quality of being certain of your abilities or of having trust in people, plans, or the future (Cambridge Dictionary, 2025)." Each one of us has the ability to tap into the power that will allow us to sustain joyfully uplifting ourselves and others in the early childhood community to create positive change. It begins with us and our commitment to stay the course and persevere during the times when it looks like our garden is not producing the fruits of our labor.

My journey in management began in my teens in retail, which later developed into my first career. I loved retail so much that I went to The Fashion Institute of Design & Merchandising, where I received my associate's degree in visual merchandising. That season of managing taught me how to have a plan and align it with company vision and meet the company's target goals. Looking back, I realized that there were interpersonal skills I needed to develop, such as empathy, diplomacy, and patience for each employee's personal situations outside work. I was trained to meet the needs of the organization, and I felt if I displayed these attributes I would not be taken advantage of. I lacked confidence in balancing hard and soft skills aligned with company goals. For instance, when I was a store manager I remember being very strict about checking pockets for security tags. I would place different prizes in each pocket of the garment to ensure that pockets were checked. It may have looked like I was being kind, but I was really showing my frustration. I would say (in a strong tone), "We are not leaving until we find the surprises in each section!" My intentions were good, but the impact was negative. My job was to drive sales, pump up my team, and reduce shrink (loss of inventory). If you have worked retail, you may relate to my experience. A retail manager's job can be related to a director's position.

As a director you drive sales with enrollment, you support your team, and you build them up to be the best teachers, while your team works together to reduce disenrollments. Even if you have different roles in the early childhood community, ideally the goal is to have a thriving workforce. Throughout these chapters we have introduced you to how to uplift yourself and your team through implementing strategies, creating environments, and facilitating family engagements. In this chapter you will be introduced to managing with confidence while continuing to uplift your team. As you read this chapter, consider how you will sustain an uplifting team and manage with confidence.

Iris's Story

Iris's journey as the new director at the Children's Garden began rocky; however, over time she began to see the rewards of her dedication. The teachers and her administrative team (Iris, Pam, and Rosa) have been reflecting on how they will continue uplifting their team joyfully. During a leadership meeting Iris thanked Rosa and Pam for the support they had given her to create an environment where they all could feel like they mattered. Iris was curious and wanted to know if they felt confident in uplifting and managing with confidence when they were managing the team by themselves. Iris was preparing to go on a vacation with her friend Jada and wanted to ensure that they would feel confident while she was away. She began with a question.

Iris: How confident do you feel about managing the team with the changes that have been put in place?

Pam: I feel good about our vision and the implementation of self-care, the makeover of the staff lounge, and connecting with families and our family engagements.

Rosa: I feel pretty good, but I am a little worried about when you go on vacation. I hope the staff will continue to maintain the policies and procedures put in place this past year.

Iris: I don't think you should have any problems, but just in case, let's develop a plan so you can feel confident when you continue to uplift and lead the team.

MANAGING CHANGE

Change can be uncomfortable for most organizations because of fear of the unknown and how it will impact our team, our jobs, and our future. If change is not properly planned, the pitfalls you face can set your organization back. In fact, 70% of change initiatives fail to meet their objectives (Ewenstein et al., 2015). Confidence is a key trait for leaders navigating change effectively. Leaders who manage with confidence effectively exhibit courage, persistence, perseverance, and strong communication skills. They are open to being adaptable, resilient, strategic, and consistent within their decision making.

When leaders intentionally decide to effectively lead change initiatives, they have a great understanding of how important it is to articulate a clear vision and uplift others to move toward change. They are purposeful and invested in their team's emotional well-being and aware of how to manage their own responses in conversations. Managing with confidence as a leader means you engage team members in the process, encouraging participation, and share ownership. When setbacks arise, you approach them with open-mindedness and demonstrate resilience. As a leader, you empower your team with the tools they need to be successful, giving your team autonomy and encouraging them every step of the way to promote confidence.

When I was a childcare director, one of the big changes we (the administration) needed to manage was "callouts." Whether you are a teacher or in a leadership role, you might know this all too well. Personally, I struggled with having a balance of sensitivity for each staff member's situation, the program needs, and enforcing the attendance policy. One reason I grappled with this was that I remember what it was like to be an early childhood teacher. At the beginning of my career in early childhood education, I was a newly single mom of three children, and I felt that there was always something coming up, or my children would get sick, causing me to call out of work or arrive late many times.

Although I had experience managing people, as a director it took some time for me to find my footing. I wanted to support my team when they were sick and when life presented them with many obstacles. I did not want to overwork the team members that were showing up for their shifts consistently and upholding the policy and procedures of the organization. To meet this challenge, I met with my leadership team to brainstorm and find some solutions. We came up with some strategies and presented them at the next staff meeting. We went over the attendance policy and the importance of showing up for each shift. Additionally, we let our team know we completely understood how life situations can impact the workplace. We expressed how we were there to partner with them and create a schedule that would meet their needs as well as the center's needs. We introduced an individual monthly communication log that would allow them to keep track of days out to the center and late arrivals. The log referenced the attendance policy on how many occurrences they could have in the annual period. The expectations and policy were clear and left room for the team to talk with us when they had a problem regarding their attendance. I found that we were successful managing change with confidence and uplifting our team when they needed it. During this process I learned how important it is to be confident in my decisions as a director and not feel guilty about doing my job.

PAUSE AND REFLECT

- How can managing with confidence impact your team?
- What barriers do you face when managing change?

TOP REASONS CHANGE INITIATIVES FAIL

In this section you will be introduced to key factors that can potentially create shortfalls as you try to implement change initiatives.

- *Lack of clear vision:* Your team does not understand the purpose of the direction of the change, or the change clashes with core values, traditions, or unspoken norms of the organization (Simpson, 2025).
- *Staff overwhelmed:* Staff are often asked to take on the change initiative on top of their regular job responsibilities, ultimately leading to burnout, disengagement, and resistance to change.
- *Lack of dedicated leadership:* Change efforts without a leader who values and understands the change initiative tend to lose momentum. If the leadership team is not visibly on board with the change, staff members are less likely to engage in the change.
- *Poor communication:* Inconsistent or unclear messages can create confusion or fear, start rumors, create resistance, and undermine trust among team members.
- *Lack of structured approach:* Change efforts without a defined process or framework tend to flounder or stall. In addition, without tracking outcomes or adjustments, strategies may set you back in your progress.

- *Insufficient support and resources:* When staff are not given sufficient time, tools, material, or effective training, change initiatives rarely succeed. For example, there were times as a director when I felt like it was impossible to give the teachers the time they needed for planning and/or meeting their professional development requirements.
- *Inadequate follow-through:* Change efforts require mechanisms for tracking progress and adjustments along the way. Without follow-through on the framework and strategies implemented, change initiatives will fizzle out.

Other reasons change initiatives fail include a lack of vision, staff not understanding "why" they are being asked to make the changes, fear, uncertainty, and attachment to the norm. Another cause is "change fatigue," which happens when there are too many changes that are happening at once, causing team members to feel overwhelmed and disengaged.

PAUSE AND REFLECT

- How many of these failed change initiative examples resonate with you?
- Take a moment to reflect on any change initiative failures you've experienced. What would you like to work on with your team?

A GARDEN HAS PURPOSE

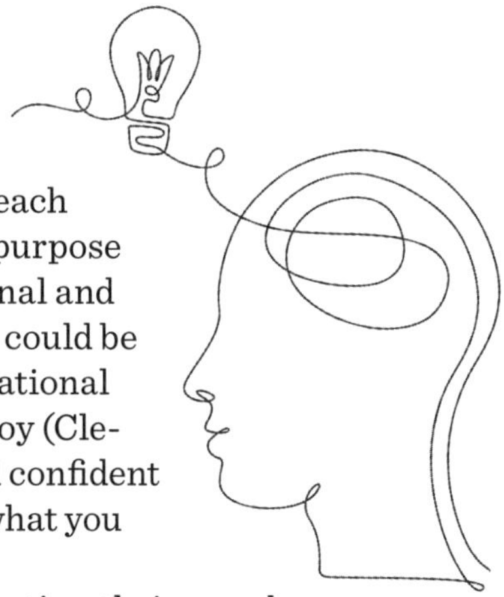

Managing change with confidence takes focus and intentionality. As I mentioned in Chapter 4, I do not have a green thumb, but I really love the aesthetics of each garden I have experienced throughout the years. The purpose of a garden can be multifaceted and can include personal and environmental benefits (Clemente, 2022). Its purpose could be food production; environmental, therapeutic, or recreational purposes, or to aesthetically pleasing for people to enjoy (Clemente, 2022). As a gardener, being knowledgeable and confident about the garden you want to plant sets the stage for what you need to be successful.

A garden can serve a person individually by boosting their mood and increasing their serotonin (Krosofsky, 2020). Research has shown that gardens and gardening activities can impact one's physical and mental health (Clemente, 2022). A garden also can enhance social skills and physical activity while contributing to biodiversity by providing a habitat for various species of insects, birds, and other animals (Clemente, 2022; Krosofsky, 2020). The gardener and the garden have a purpose and a vision to produce and to sustain what has been cultivated. As leaders, we possess the same powers with uplifting and managing with confidence in our programs. It begins with us. Managing with confidence is purposeful. Having a clear plan, like the gardener, will help you develop your team and program. Below are some strategies to improve the success rate of change initiatives.

STRATEGIES TO IMPROVE CHANGE INITIATIVE SUCCESS

Share the "Vision"

Communicate with your team a clear vision that aligns with organizational goals, mission, and values. When working by yourself or with other administrators, create a vision that shares the "why" behind change in simple and inspiring language. Remember, there is purpose when you're planning a garden. Be intentional. Paint a picture of what the future will look like if the change initiatives are successful. Use simple messaging to define what success will look like and to build trust with your children, teachers, and families. For example, discuss old systems and share how the new system works to support them. Anchor decisions in your shared values. This provides stability during uncertainty.

Designate a Change Leader or Leadership Team

Appoint a dedicated leader or team to guide and manage the process from start to finish. Give your team the time and tools they will need to be successful with the change initiative. Be open and invite input and feedback about what's working and where you will need to make changes. Using your team creates involvement and boosts ownership and reduces resistance.

Courage Over Discomfort

Create a courageous sense of optimism. Prepare your team using conversations to express the discomfort they will feel during the process of change. Remain calm and solution-focused, showing confidence in uncertainty, pause and listen, and clarify the problem. Model calm, confident leadership while

expressing hope and competence. For instance, this could be a one-on-one conversation during a check-in with your assistant director or during a team meeting.

Model Change

Demonstrate through action by modeling what you want to see (Simpson, 2025). There was a phrase growing up that I heard a lot: "Do as I say not as I do." As a leader managing change with confidence, you want to model the change and have your team "do as I do." For example, if you would like your classrooms to be clutter free, the administration workspace should be clutter free. It will inspire and uplift your team, and they will believe in what you have told them.

Be Proactive and Involve Others

Be aware of the possible problems that may arise and partner with your team to embrace new solutions at each phase of the change initiative (Bodell, 2022). Build new behaviors into existing workflows to help them stick for instance, creating well-wishes for teachers that have called out sick. Callouts are common in early childhood programs and have the potential to impact morale within the organization. By being proactive and involving team members to create well-wishes, you can change how callouts are viewed from a negative to a positive and with empathy and support.

Provide Emotional Support and Encouragement

Check in with your team often. Be aware of the support your team needs to be successful. Offer ways for them to express their emotions. Check in with your team to see if they need support with completing their task. Foster flexibility, curiosity, and building a culture that embraces making positive changes. Tackle changes incrementally to prevent burnout: one situation at a time.

Be Trauma Informed

Trauma is an uncomfortable reality that we face in the early childhood community. We as individuals may carry our own personal trauma, our staff may experience job trauma, and the children and families we serve may have been exposed to trauma in their home life. "Trauma has no boundaries regarding age, gender, socioeconomic status, race, ethnicity, or sexual orientation (SAMHSA, 2025)." As a leader, we can recognize the frequency of trauma in the world and seek to be responsive to this unfortunate reality (King, 2021). When your team is experiencing the effects of trauma, managing with confidence will be a hard task. The first step is to have informational training sessions on being trauma informed and have professionals as guest speakers at your team meetings and family engagements. Create a space to have safe conversations, with resources available. Take the time to find out what the needs are in your program. Be present and observant. For example, if you find that one of your team members is always late, take the time to find out why with care and concern. Another example might be a staff member who is quiet and isolates themselves but does not know how to get help. You are only as successful as your team.

Celebrate Small Wins

Recognize and celebrate small wins to maintain positive momentum and morale. Highlight strengths and reassure your team, "We're in this together." Encourage your team to seek out what is working during this initiative.

Be Visible and Transparent

Be an active part of the team and the change initiative. Provide ongoing updates and communicate them early and often, even when you have to communicate hard things. For example, this could be through monthly emails, team newsletters, or group messaging.

PAUSE AND REFLECT

- What two strategies are you willing to try?
- How can you celebrate the small wins when managing with confidence?

CALL TO ACTION

Uplifting others and managing with confidence will not be an easy task. Train, model, and praise your team with intentionality. I know, I keep using "intentional" and "intentionality" because they are action words. It means that you believe in this work to support uplifting others by managing with confidence. Create an action plan using TMP (train, model, and praise).

Train

Train your administrative team on the strategies to improve change initiatives successfully. Review them and revise them to fit your program. Schedule a training series for each change initiative strategy. For instance, when using the "share the vision" strategy, you could create three mini 1-hour sessions: organizational goal, mission, and values. Create space for your team to add their ideas to each session.

Model

Model the strategies to improve change initiatives with your administrative team using examples and role-play at their comfort level. Some of your team members may not be comfortable role-playing in front of others. Be open and flexible and give them choices on how they would like to model the strategies, one on one or in real time in a classroom. Remember, as a leader managing change with confidence, you want to model the change and have your team "do as I do."

Praise

Take the time to check in with your admin team to praise them on what is going well to build their confidence. Provide positive descriptive feedback and focus on the actions. Avoid saying the words "good job" without identifying what you observed that was done well. As a coach and coordinator, my team and the teachers I coach have expressed how positive descriptive feedback helps them feel confident when doing their job. Everyone loves to hear when they are doing a wonderful job. It builds confidence. In Figure 9.1 you will find a completed example of the "TMP (Train, Model, and Parise) Planning Document." See Appendix C for a reproducible version.

Iris's Approach

Iris took the time to go over the possible pitfalls they could face as a team. She reviewed the top change initiatives that fail within an organization. Then she asked Rosa and Pam the following question:

Iris: Rosa and Pam, what do you think we might encounter out of the top reasons change initiatives failed?

Rosa: I think we could do better with our follow-through. We had a good pace, but I feel since we have become busy it's been tough to circle back around with the teachers. And to be honest, it's hard for me to have tough conversations with the teachers. I would like to save those conversations for you, Iris.

Pam: I would agree with Rosa. Although we have been here for a while, the last couple of directors took care of all the management. We did the minimal and were placed in the classrooms to support the teacher much of the time.

Iris: Thank you for being transparent. I want you to know that I am confident I can guide and support you to manage with confidence. Let's go over the strategies to improve change initiatives successfully.

Iris and the leadership team went through the strategies and began to talk about how they could use each one. Iris used examples they had all experienced, and she role-played with them at their comfort level.

Iris: Rosa and Pam, your participation and your responses within the scenarios leave me with a good feeling that you will do well in supporting the continued changes with confidence.

THE JOYFUL UPLIFT DIFFERENCE

Uplifting others and managing with confidence for me is a blend of my retail management experience and managing in the early childhood field. Sustainability within your program will require you to be consistent with managing change with confidence. These two skills (uplifting others and managing with confidence) blend well. Managing with confidence fosters an environment where the team you lead can grow in a way that produces fruits to uplift the teachers, families, and children you serve. Although within my career I have made mistakes and experienced failures, I have learned how to trust myself and my team to uplift others and manage with confidence.

INDIVIDUAL REFLECTION

1. Do you manage and lead your team with confidence?
2. How do you support your administration team to manage with confidence?
3. What does uplifting others and managing with confidence mean to you?

BOOK GROUP OR CLASSROOM DISCUSSION

1. Is it hard for you to use courage over comfort when faced with change? Why or why not?
2. What current strategies do you have in place to use when staff become overwhelmed?
3. How can you be a leader that manages change with confidence?

UPLIFT IN ACTION

Select one or more of the following to practice Uplift in Action.

- Create an action plan using train, model, and praise (TMP)
- Check in with your administrative team to see if they need support managing with confidence.
- Continue to share the vision, goals, progress, and challenges during the change initiatives.
- Encourage feedback and active participation.

TMP

Train, Model, and Praise

Planning Document

TRAIN Identify the strategy/ies to train on to drive the current change initiative.

Strategy Change Initiative: Courage over discomfort.

MODEL Detail the specific actions you will take to model the strategy/ies. How would you like to model the strategy/ies? One on One or Real Time (office/classroom/group setting). Circle preference.

I will train and model for Rosa on conversations that she deems uncomfortable. Rosa would like to have one-on-one modeling sessions with scenarios of her choice. I will also invite Rosa to observe any conversations that I may have with team members to model calmness, pause and listen, clarify the problem with team members, and work with them to identify a solution(s).

PRAISE Plan and provide positive descriptive feedback when staff is observed using the specific change initiative strategy/ies.

Rosa demonstrated calmness and created a safe environment for staff who experienced a parent complaint. I will tell her, "Rosa, I was so impressed by the calm and composed way you handled the parent complaint. You help create a safe space for the staff by engaging in respectful and productive conversation. Which helped everyone feel more at ease. I am grateful to have someone like you guiding our team."

*Evaluate the effectiveness of strategy/ies change initiative implemented.

Figure 9.1. "Train, Model, and Praise (TMP) Planning Document" example (reproducible blank version is available on the Brookes Download Hub).

10

The Ripple Effect of Joyful Uplift: Be the Light

Teresa Byington

As we conclude our journey focused on joyfully uplifting ourselves and others, this final chapter will serve as your guide to implementing these practices into your leadership repertoire. We'll explore how you can be the light that creates a ripple effect of positivity in your leadership and beyond.

Throughout this book, we've explored what it means to uplift yourself and others using a gardening theme. Once the soil is prepared and the seeds are planted, it is time to step fully into Uplift in Action. How have people demonstrated Uplift in Action in your life? Did they engage in small acts of uplift such as giving you a gift of appreciation or sharing words of gratitude that made a big difference in how you felt? Did they provide uplifting support and comfort during a difficult time? These are examples of Uplift in Action that brings light and joy into someone else's life. As the following quote, commonly attributed to the Buddha, sums up, encouragement and kindness can ignite hope in others without diminishing your own light. "Thousands of candles can be lighted from a single candle, and the life of the candle will not be shortened. Happiness never decreases by being shared" (Hanh, 1991). We can increase our own happiness and joy by sharing it with others. In fact, everyone can be an

uplifting leader, even if they do not have a specific leadership role. Early childhood educators are leaders in their classroom, and they can be empowered to tap into their leadership abilities by joyfully uplifting others!

BE THE GARDENER OF JOYFUL UPLIFT: POSITIVE RELATIONAL ENERGY

Joyful, uplifting leadership is intentional. It is becoming a gardener of joyful uplift through daily actions that include planting hope when someone is tired, watering confidence when a team member is unsure, and pulling weeds of negativity with compassion and care. Joyful, uplifting leaders have what Jamie Shapiro calls positive relational energy, which is the energy that occurs during interactions (Shapiro, 2024). When someone goes away from an interaction feeling energized, they have experienced positive relational energy. The opposite is also true. When someone leaves an interaction feeling drained, they have experienced negative relational energy.

As shared in Chapter 2, it is beneficial for leaders to prioritize their own well-being so they have the energy to be an uplifting influence. When leaders interact with positive relational energy, they can have a great impact on a team member's performance. Leaders bringing their uplifting energy into the workplace create a ripple effect that positively impacts others. Think about a time when you felt energized during an interaction. What was happening? Who were you with? What impacted the energy level of the interaction? How can you bring more positive relational energy to your interactions?

Becoming a Pollinator of Possibility

Joyful, uplifting leadership is more than just encouraging or motivating others. It involves seeing each person's potential, giving them opportunities to grow, and then continuing to help them flourish (Untitled Leader, 2024). Just as bees carry pollen, your uplift carries power across your team, your program, and your community. Your actions may seem small, but their impact is far-reaching. Your leadership requires a balance of support, where individuals feel empowered and guided, and accountable, ensuring that they are challenged to meet expectations and learn from mistakes. Uplifting leadership will be the most impactful when it becomes embedded into the culture of an organization. Uplift in Action is not a set of isolated actions but rather an environment that positively impacts every interaction and experience within an organization. Embracing Uplift in Action often leads to higher levels of team engagement, increased innovation, and improved retention rates.

A Call to Cultivate Lasting Change

As we have explored throughout the book, leaders have opportunities every day to model uplift, nurture it in others, and embed it into the culture of their programs. When you uplift others, you offer hope for a brighter future; you are cultivating lasting change. Effective leaders offer grace when mistakes happen, celebrate effort, not just outcomes, and invest in relational trust, not just compliance. Uplifting leaders know the difference between knowing and doing. They have the courage to put Uplift in Action even when going through tough times.

The world seems brighter when engaging in uplifting actions. You will feel closer to the people receiving the positive actions and feel better about yourself. A poem attributed to Henry Wadsworth Longfellow says, "Kind hearts are the gardens. Kind thoughts are the roots. Kind words are the blossoms. Kind deeds are the fruits. Take care of your garden and keep out the weeds, Fill it with sunshine, kind words and kind deeds" (Longfellow, n.d.). Isn't that a beautiful metaphor? We truly can have a beautiful life garden when we have kind hearts and kind thoughts and engage in uplifting actions. Our thoughts become our words, and our words become our deeds. How much better the world would be if more people focused on being kind to others and to themselves. It is also important to give yourself some grace when things do not go as well as planned.

THE RIPPLE EFFECT OF UPLIFT: HARVEST AND REPLANT

Every act of uplift sends ripples. Like a stone dropped in a still pond, uplift doesn't stop where it lands. It moves outward, reaching people we may never see. Acts of uplift begin a ripple that spreads. Your daily actions are planting the future, and soon you will see how the fruits of your labor have become the harvest of joyful uplift. You may see a teacher who smiles more freely, feeling seen and supported, team members that trust each other more deeply, and classrooms filled with laughter and joy. Celebrate moments when your leadership helped someone bloom, and share stories that remind others that joy matters. Remember, the harvest isn't the end; it's the beginning of the next season. To lead with uplift is to replant again and again with hope. Replant after a hard conversation; replant after a staff change; replant when others have forgotten the power of joyful uplift.

Every season is a chance to renew your purpose and continue to grow, because although many leaders intend to uplift others, the daily demands of busyness, stress, or other challenges can often stand in the way. There is an

ongoing need to be intentional about planting seeds of resilience, confidence, and joy. These seeds are sown through a warm smile, a kind word, a gentle redirection, or a moment of deep listening. Here are several ways leaders can emulate Uplift in Action and create a ripple effect.

IRIS'S STORY—PLANT IT FORWARD: FIVE PRACTICES OF UPLIFTING LEADERS

Just as a gardener tends to soil, light, and water, uplifting leaders practice daily care, because a single seed planted with intention can grow a garden of transformation. To put Uplift in Action, leaders can plant it forward by focusing on these five practices, the seeds of lasting impact.

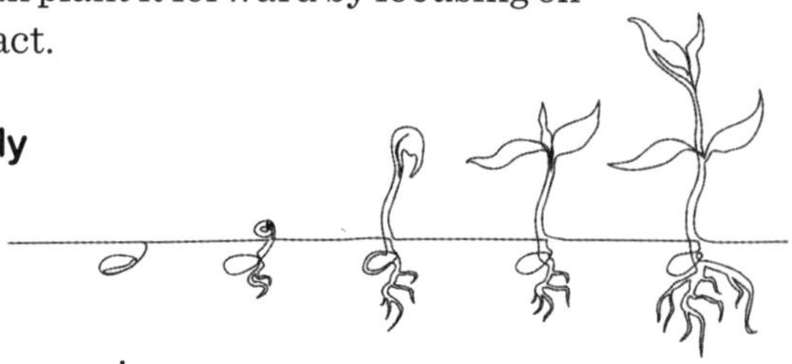

1. See the Good and Spot the Sprouts Early

Watch for new growth. Look for what is working. Uplifting leaders notice the strengths in their team members, families, and children. Seeing the good does not mean you ignore problems; instead, you focus on possibilities. These leaders see potential in others and strive to nurture the latent abilities in the individuals they lead. Recognize the effort, not just the achievement. Speak hope during difficult moments.

During a stressful licensing visit, Iris kept her cool. Instead of panicking, she checked in with each teacher, offered snacks in the break room, and told her teachers, "We are in this together; I see the awesome work you do every day." Her team reported feeling seen and supported.

Uplift in Action: Plant it forward

- Write a thank-you note to one of your team members.
- Tell a team member something specific you admire about them.
- Share the strength of one of your team members during a staff meeting.

2. Communicate to Elevate With Words of Sunshine

Uplifting leaders communicate with clarity, curiosity, and care. Words are spoken with warmth and kindness. These leaders are aware of the tone and timing of their words. They focus on the effort, not just the outcome, giving feedback that feels like fertilizer, nourishing and growth focused.

Iris asked her team to create bulletin boards that highlighted the children in their classroom. She told Shannon and Mei, "I noticed how much care you put into choosing materials for your bulletin board that reflected each child's family and culture. This shows deep intentionality. Thank you for your efforts."

Uplift in Action: Plant it forward

- Begin each day by giving your team members warm, personal greetings.
- Say something kind to someone you don't usually connect with.
- Give someone a shout-out for helping others.

3. Hold Space and Be the Trellis

Uplifting leaders create emotionally safe and inclusive environments, just as the trellis gives plants structure to grow. These leaders hold safe, supportive space where others can stretch, try, stumble, and bloom. They are a calm and compassionate presence. These leaders strive to be fully present, emotionally steady, and nonjudgmental, especially during moments of vulnerability. Holding space includes setting emotionally safe boundaries for everyone. Leaders demonstrate authentic vulnerability by admitting a mistake and sharing a challenge they've overcome. These actions can build deeper trust and encourage others to be more open.

Carla came into Iris's office visually upset. Iris invited her to sit down and share what was troubling her. Carla vented about her co-teacher with intense emotion. Iris responded, "I hear that you are upset. Let's focus on what you need and how I can support you." Iris was able to gently steer the conversation away from blame and toward what Carla needed.

The interactions that leaders have with team members during emotionally charged conversations demonstrate whether team members feel emotionally safe. Team members may be reluctant to share how they really feel about something if they have been shut down in the past. Leaders that embrace the motto of "my way or the highway" are not promoting emotional safety within their teams. Emotional safety is built over time. Become more aware of how team members feel in your presence.

Uplift in Action: Plant it forward

- Offer a listening ear to a team member without giving advice.
- Create a cozy, calming space in your break room.
- Take a slow deep breath before responding to a challenge.

4. Celebrate Progress and Harvest Joy Along the Way

Uplifting leaders acknowledge small wins and growth in others. They do not wait until the final bloom to celebrate. They harvest joy as it comes by honoring growth in every stage. These leaders normalize mistakes as part of growth. They realize the most meaningful celebrations are often thoughtful and heartfelt. Adding elements of surprise and specificity can often lead to joyful celebrations.

Iris created an "I Saw You Shine" board in the break room. She surprised the teachers with a personal note that celebrated each person. For Maria the note read, "I saw you shine when you welcomed a new child to your classroom with such warmth." For Alex she wrote, "I saw you shine when you shared your sensory bin ideas, and it inspired three other teachers to implement your ideas!"

Uplift in Action: Plant it forward

- Celebrate small wins from the week with your team.
- Recognize a quiet hero on your team.
- Post a quote about joy or growth where others will see it.

5. Stand for Joy and Be the Light that Keeps the Garden Growing

Uplifting leaders choose joy and model resilience. They know joy is essential. To stand for joy means to choose to lead with optimism, hope, and intentional actions. It means making time to cultivate light, laughter, and connection. Leaders stand for joy by infusing humor into routines, such as sharing a fun meme or asking, "What made a child laugh today?" or "What brought you joy?" They add light and keep the garden growing with joy.

Iris adapted the practice of sharing "uplift sprinkles" on Fridays. These uplift sprinkles were short stories about something beautiful or funny that happened in the program. Her team could also share uplift sprinkles. Iris shared, "I overheard a child tell her mom, 'My teacher helped me be brave today.' The child's mother hugged her and told her how proud she was of her. Our uplift sprinkle is celebrating all the teachers who create joy by helping a child take a leap of bravery."

Infuse humor by sharing fun stories with each other that are joyful. A teacher shared that on her first day in an early childhood classroom, she had taken the children to lunch. Everyone seemed to be focused on eating their lunch, until she noticed one little boy was taking all his clothes off. She went over and asked him what he was doing. He said that he would be in big trouble if he got his clothes dirty, and he didn't want to get any food on his clothes. The teacher told him that was very smart thinking, but he could keep his clothes on, and she would get him some extra napkins to keep his clothes clean.

Uplift in Action: Plant it forward

- Protect joy as a vital part of your culture. Start the day with joyful energy, do a short dance to upbeat music, or take a short walk outside to connect with nature.
- Create a joyful playlist of songs that lift your mood and share it with your team. Then invite your team to add their favorite songs to the playlist.
- Choose one routine and add a joyful twist, such as adding music to arrival time.

PAUSE AND REFLECT

- What kind of uplifter do you want to be remembered as?
- What would your organization be like if Uplift in Action was a daily practice?
- What uplifting actions could you implement this week?

WEEDS AND WEATHER: TOUGH CHALLENGES IN YOUR GARDEN OF UPLIFT

Every leader who commits to uplifting themselves and others will face obstacles just as gardeners face weeds and weather. Some challenges may be external, and others may grow from within. When you are struggling with challenges that are preventing you from engaging in Uplift in Action, it can be helpful to learn about the experiences of others. Here are two examples of individuals that overcame challenges and uplifted others.

Chris Singleton, a former professional baseball player for the Chicago Cubs, is one powerful example of someone who demonstrated Uplift in Action when faced with immense challenges (Fisher, 2019). His mother was murdered at her church in South Carolina. Following her death, Chris began spreading the message that "love is stronger than hate." He said, "You can't control everything that happens to you in life. You can only control how you respond." Chris Singleton is an exceptional example of transforming your outlook. Instead of wallowing in anger and hate, he focused on love. He made a positive choice in how he decided to react to an extremely sad and difficult life experience. His response to a difficult situation had a powerful impact on others. Chris's choice to focus on love instead of hate prevented others from engaging in violence and revenge. His actions helped to heal hearts and bring a community together in love. He is an example of how focusing on uplifting others can have powerful outcomes.

The second person that has had a far-reaching positive impact on others is Jon Gordon, author of *The Energy Bus* (2007) and *The Power of Positive Leadership* (2017). Jon's story begins with him mired in negativity. His negativity was so profound that it threatened both his marriage and employment. The severity of his situation caused him to do some deep reflection, and he realized that what he was doing was not working. When he flipped his mindset and slowly began to focus on positivity and joy, his world changed! His journey was not without setbacks and struggles, but he was persistent. Now his message of positivity reaches thousands through his books, podcasts, and "Power of Positive" summits. He has made a difference in his work by focusing on uplifting others. There are many examples of Uplift in Action that can inspire us in our work. Who has inspired you?

Like a dedicated gardener, you don't abandon the garden when things get tough. Instead, you tend it, you weed it, you water it, and you protect it. Find your garden allies and build momentum with a few. Keep focused on your roots (purpose) of joy and uplift.

SIGNS OF A THRIVING GARDEN: HOW TO KNOW IF UPLIFT IN ACTION IS WORKING

You may be wondering, how do I know if Uplift in Action is working? When a garden starts to flourish, you see new buds, richer soil, and fewer pests. The same is true with Uplift in Action. Here are some things you may see.

Changes in team dynamics:

- *Increased collaboration:* Team members are more willing to help each other, share ideas, and work together on projects. They seek opportunities to collaborate and look for opportunities to share ideas with others.
- *More open communication:* Team members are more comfortable sharing concerns, ideas, and even mistakes without fear of judgment. You will observe more active listening and less interrupting in meetings.

- *Positive relational energy in interactions:* Conversations will feel lighter, more energized, and less draining. You will see more smiles and hear more laughter.
- *Constructive conflict resolution:* When disagreements arise, they are handled constructively, with team members focusing on solutions rather than blame.

Hearing positive feedback:

- *Informal comments:* Listen for spontaneous expressions of gratitude, appreciation, or positive experiences from team members. These small remarks often indicate a shift in atmosphere.
- *Direct feedback:* When team members are asked specific questions such as "What makes you feel most supported here?" or "When do you feel most energized by our team?" they share examples about how they feel supported and uplifted.
- *Stories shared:* Team members start sharing stories about their own uplifting actions or how they've felt uplifted by others. These stories indicate the ripple effect is taking hold.

Positive indicators:

- *Retention rates:* A more uplifting environment often leads to lower turnover as people feel more connected and fulfilled.
- *Innovation and idea generation:* An emotionally safe and uplifting environment encourages people to take risks and share new ideas. Are you seeing more creative solutions or suggestions?
- *Less absenteeism:* A positive environment can contribute to lower absenteeism and team members being more fully engaged when at work.

Self-reflection and your own feelings:

- *Your energy levels:* Do you feel more energized and joyful in your leadership role? This is a strong indicator that your efforts are creating a positive feedback loop.
- *Sense of connection:* Do you feel more connected to your team and the impact you're having?
- *"Lightness" in the workplace:* Does the overall atmosphere feel lighter, more hopeful, and less burdened by negativity?

Iris's Approach

Iris looked out the window at the sun shining on the blooming tulips and thought about how things had not always been this sunny and bright. Iris had spent several years planting seeds of change and had worked through many difficult situations. Over time the atmosphere at The Children's Garden had shifted. As she walked down the hall, she heard more laughter than complaints. Her team had learned how to listen, reflect, and solve problems together. Disagreements still bubbled up from time to time, but her team was willing to have tough conversations and find workable solutions. There was more positive energy and collaboration, as team members helped each other prepare a last-minute art project or clean up after a family event. Iris smiled as she watched her team laughing with the children, exchanging ideas, and being playful. Iris realized she felt light and joyful. The energy she used to spend putting out fires was now spent fueling connections with her team and the children and families at their center.

KEEP TENDING THE GARDEN AS YOU CONTINUE THE JOURNEY

To sustain a culture of joy, uplift, kindness, and growth, leaders must keep tending the garden and themselves. The following are some ideas on how you can continue your journey of continuous growth and ongoing uplift.

Keep watering your roots and prioritize your own well-being:

- *Consistent self-care:* Continue to prioritize your own energy and joy. Refer to Chapter 2 for specific practices such as mindfulness, hobbies, time in nature, and connecting with your own support system that help you care for yourself.
- *Learning and growth:* Uplift is not a destination; it is an ongoing journey. Engage in continuous learning about positive psychology, emotional intelligence, and leadership best practices. Read books, attend workshops, and listen to podcasts.

Welcome the rain by seeking and embracing feedback (your own uplift):

- *Regular check-ins:* Schedule brief, informal check-ins with trusted colleagues, mentors, or team members where you specifically ask for feedback on your uplifting efforts. "How am I doing at creating a positive environment?" "What could I do better?"
- *Practice receiving feedback gracefully:* Model how to receive feedback with openness and curiosity, even when it's challenging.

Spread the seeds by becoming an uplift ambassador:

- *Mentor others:* Share your experiences and insights with aspiring leaders. Mentor colleagues on how to cultivate uplift in their own teams.

- *Share your stories:* Continue to share joyful stories within your organization. Celebrate uplifting actions you witness in others, inspiring them to do the same.
- *Advocate for uplift:* Champion the principles of uplifting leadership within your organization's culture, policies, and practices.

Make it part of the soil by integrating uplift into daily routines:

- *Combine habits:* Link uplifting actions to existing daily habits. For example, every time you check your email, send one quick note of appreciation.
- *Scheduled "uplift moments":* Intentionally block out time for small acts of uplift, whether it's a quick walk-around to connect with team members or taking time for a meaningful conversation.

Not every seed sprouts: Embrace the imperfect journey:

- *Grace for yourself:* Remind yourself that nobody is perfect. There will be days when things don't go as planned. Give yourself grace and refocus. Remember, you do what you can with what you have and know.
- *Resilience and adaptability:* Uplifting leadership is about choosing to bring light even during challenges. Remember, the journey will have its ups and downs, but the commitment to uplift is what matters.

Grow in a grove and connect with a community of uplifters:

- *Peer support:* Find other leaders who are committed to similar principles. Share experiences, challenges, and successes.
- *Professional networks:* Join groups or communities focused on positive leadership or organizational culture.

THE NEXT CHAPTER: IRIS THE JOYFUL UPLIFT AMBASSADOR

Iris realized that uplift wasn't a project; it was a way of leading. A way of living. She had learned over time that in order to pour into others, her own cup had to be full. She had made a commitment to take care of herself. She started each day with a quiet moment on her porch. Every Friday afternoon, she went for a walk through the nearby park. She had rediscovered her love for gardening. She often reminded herself, "Joy starts with me." Iris knew her leadership was more effective when she was joyful and uplifted others. She had learned to welcome feedback as she continued her journey of growth.

Over time, word of the transformation at The Children's Garden started to spread. Directors from other centers reached out to Iris, and she invited them to visit the center. Soon Iris was informally mentoring other early childhood leaders on how to build a culture of positivity and connection. She started sharing practical tips for positive leadership and was asked to present at a state conference. At the conference, Iris shared how she had woven uplift into her daily life by creating tiny rituals. After checking her email each morning, she sent one quick thank-you or note of encouragement to one of her team members. On Wednesdays, she did a "smile walk" around the center, popping into classrooms to say hello and notice something joyful. Once a month, her team was invited to join a 15-minute care circle of gratitude where they could share a shout-out or celebration. These small moments had made a difference.

Not surprisingly, not every day was light. There were moments of tension, hard conversations with families, and days when she was exhausted, but Iris had learned to give herself the same grace she offered others. She had written herself a note, which she read frequently. The note said, "Show up with heart in good times and bad." One good thing that had strengthened her was the community of uplifting leaders that she had formed with a small group of directors. They met monthly and shared strategies and offered each other encouragement as they laughed (and sometimes cried) together. They reminded each other of the big picture of leading with light even when clouds roll in.

Iris felt like she had come full circle when she walked past the toddler room and saw two teachers giggling over a cup of coffee and a lesson plan covered in glitter. A sticky note on the door read, "You are the sunshine!" She smiled. The seeds had taken root. The garden was blooming.

PAUSE AND REFLECT

- Who will you uplift today?
- How will you make a positive difference in your circle of influence?

YOUR UPLIFT LEADERSHIP LEGACY: WHAT WILL YOUR GARDEN GROW?

It is your time to create your own uplift leadership legacy. You can do this by intentionally cultivating a lasting impact that inspires growth and confidence in others. As an uplifting leader, the impact you sow today will bloom in the hearts, minds, and lives of others long after your footsteps have left the garden path. Think about what you want people to remember and how you want them to feel. Then write a personal uplift statement by filling in the blanks.

As a leader, I choose to uplift others by __________________ because I believe ________________________.

Here are our examples:

Teresa Byington

"As a leader, I choose to uplift others by encouraging playfulness and connection because I believe a joyful environment inspires creativity, engagement, and resilience."

Geraldine "Gigi" Wynn

"As a leader, I choose to uplift others by providing a space to learn from mistakes and inspire people to reach their goals because I believe in you."

Danielle Pertile

"As a leader, I choose to uplift others by celebrating wins both big and small, because I believe that even the smallest accomplishments are a step toward growth."

Charmika "Mika" Hansen

"As a leader, I choose to uplift others by leading with joy, empathy, and curiosity because I believe a positive and inclusive environment unlocks the very best of what is in our hearts."

You will leave an uplifting legacy as your daily actions reflect kindness, curiosity, and integrity. Uplifting leaders share their knowledge generously and care more about what they leave behind than who gets the applause. They have learned how to grow alongside their team and receive feedback with grace and openness. One of your most defining moments will be how you respond under pressure. Exemplify grace under fire. This means maintaining composure, empathy, and a focus on positive solutions even when faced with significant adversity.

THE JOYFUL UPLIFT DIFFERENCE: THE BLOOMS THAT CARRY ON

Remember, you are enough. As an uplifting leader you will shine brightly and leave a positive impact on the individuals whose lives you touch. Think about the beautiful garden you are creating as you uplift yourself and others. You will bring joy into your life and the lives of others as you exemplify Uplift in Action!

INDIVIDUAL REFLECTION

1. Think about a time you experienced "positive relational energy." What specifically happened, and how did it make you feel? How can you intentionally create more of these moments in your daily interactions?

2. Review the five practices of uplifting leaders. Which practice resonates most with you, and why? Which one presents the biggest challenge for you to implement, and what's one small step you can take to grow in that area?

3. Draft your personal uplift statement now: "As a leader, I choose to uplift others by __________ because I believe __________." How does this statement align with your values and aspirations for your leadership legacy?

BOOK GROUP OR DISCUSSION QUESTIONS

1. The book emphasizes that Uplift in Action is often small acts that can make a big difference. Share a personal example of how a small act of uplift, either given or received, had a significant impact on your life.
2. Discuss the five practices of uplifting leaders. Which practice do you believe is most crucial for fostering a truly uplifting team culture, and why? Are there any practices you would add or emphasize differently?
3. Thinking about the ripple effect of uplift, how can we, as a group or within our respective organizations, intentionally amplify these positive ripples beyond our immediate teams? What are some collective actions we could take?

Getting to Know Your Family
Sample Questionnaire

Welcome! We value every family's unique story and look forward to partnering with you this year. Please share as much or as little as you'd like. Your responses will help us create a supportive and inclusive classroom community.

1. **Names and Pronouns**

   Child's name:

   Preferred pronouns (optional):

2. **Who Is in Your Family?**

   Please tell us about the important people in your child's life (parents, grandparents, siblings, caregivers, or even pets etc.):

3. **Family Languages**

   What languages are spoken at home?

   Are there words or phrases (in any language) you'd like us to use with your child?

4. **Traditions and Celebrations**

   What holidays, traditions, or special events do your family celebrate?

   Would you like to share any of these with the class? (circle one):

   Yes Maybe Not currently

5. **Family Strengths and Interests**

   What do you enjoy doing together as a family?

   Are there hobbies, talents, or skills you would be interested in sharing with the class (cooking, music, gardening, art, storytelling, etc.)?

6. **Comfort and Support**

   How does your child like to be comforted when upset?

   Is there anything that helps your child feel safe and welcome?

7. **Communication Preferences**

   What's the best way for us to reach you? (circle all that apply)

   Text Email Phone Call School App Other: ____________________

8. **Family Milestones or Changes**

   Are there recent or upcoming family milestones or changes (moves, new siblings, etc.) you'd like us to know about?

9. **What else would you like us to know about your family or your child?**

10. How would you like to participate in our program this year? (Optional; select any that interest you):

- ❒ Reading to the class
- ❒ Sharing about your family's culture or traditions
- ❒ Helping at events or on field trips
- ❒ Sending in recipes, art, or photos
- ❒ Helping from home (preparing materials, making phone calls, etc.)
- ❒ Other ideas: ______________________________

____

____

____

____

Thank you for sharing! We're excited to get to know your family and build a joyful year together.

Ten Fun Family Engagement Ideas

When planning family engagement events, consider offering activities at different times such as weekday mornings, late afternoons, evenings, and weekends in order to accommodate families with varied schedules. For some events, families may also be able to contribute supplies or materials.

1. **Family Tradition Potluck**

   Invite families to bring a dish that represents their special traditions, heritage, or culture to share at a potluck or picnic. Keeping the prompt open-ended and culturally sensitive encourages creativity and results in a diverse spread of unique and meaningful dishes. Families may also write or share a short story about where the dish came from and why it is meaningful to them. It may be that a grandparent passed the recipe down to them, or it may be that they invented it by accident and it became a family favorite!

2. **Weekend Outings**

   Plan seasonal group outings, such as apple orchards in the fall, strawberry fields in the spring, or pumpkin patches in October. These low-cost outdoor experiences offer families a relaxed way to connect outside the classroom.

3. **Pizza and Games Night**

   Host an evening event with pizza and drinks and invite families to bring a favorite board or card game to share. Even if some families don't bring a game, everyone can participate and enjoy the fun.

4. **Booknic (Book + Picnic)**

   On a warm or mild day, invite families to bring lunch and a few favorite books to enjoy picnic-style in your outdoor area or playground. This simple, screen-free event promotes bonding and a shared love of reading.

5. **Coffee and Connections**

   Set up a casual morning coffee and tea station with pastries or donuts near the entrance. Parents can drop in before or after drop-off to chat with staff or connect with other families.

6. **Family Flag Day**

   Provide poster boards, magazines, glue, markers, and paint, and invite families to create a "family flag" that represents who they are. They can include elements like pets, hobbies, languages, holidays, or family traditions. Display the finished flags in classrooms or the lobby to celebrate your community's diversity.

7. **Family Art Day/Night**

   Offer a relaxed art experience with a variety of simple materials like paint, collage supplies, stamps, or recycled items. Families can create side by side or work on a shared piece to take home or display at the center.

8. **Field Day at the Park**

   Coordinate a meet-up at a nearby park. Families bring lunch and picnic blankets and enjoy outdoor activities together. Encourage families to bring along favorite play items like balls, hula hoops, chalk, or bubbles to share.

9. **Kindergarten Wish Wells**

   At the end of the school year (or end of summer), set up a station for families and children to write or draw kind messages for students transitioning to kindergarten. Display these wishes near their classrooms to celebrate the milestone and let them know they're supported by their school community.

10. **Family Makerspace Challenge**

    A makerspace is a place or event where children and families can explore a variety of materials. It is an open-ended activity where imagination, exploration, and curiosity take the forefront and there is no wrong way to play (Marx-Mackerley et al. 2021).

    In the weeks leading up to this event, collect clean, safe recyclables and "art junk" supplies like cardboard boxes, paper towel tubes, packing materials, and clean yogurt containers. Families may also choose to donate materials like pipe cleaners, popsicle sticks, paper plates, and so forth. At the event, provide building materials such as tape, glue, and scissors, and pose a design challenge such as "Build a bridge using only the materials you have available to you." The possibilities both for materials and for outcomes are endless!

    Optional: Start with a story about creativity like *Not a Box* by Antoinette Portis (2006) or *Twenty-One Elephants and Still Standing* by April Jones Prince and François Roca (2005), and then invite families to create their own imaginative "not-a-box" creations or bridges that can hold the most elephants. This open-ended activity sparks creativity, teamwork, and lots of fun for all ages.

TMP

Train, Model, and Praise

Planning Document

TRAIN: Identify the strategy/ies to train on to drive the current change initiative.

MODEL: Detail the specific actions you will take to model the strategy/ies. How would you like to model the strategy/ies? One on one or real time (office/classroom/group setting). Circle preference.

PRAISE: Plan and provide positive descriptive feedback when staff is observed using the specific change initiative strategy/ies.

*Evaluate the effectiveness of the strategy/ies change initiative implemented.

References

Adam, H., & Galinsky, A. D. (2012). Enclothed cognition. *Journal of Experimental Social Psychology, 48*(4), 918–925. https://doi.org/10.1016/j.jesp.2012.02.008

Atyah, R. (2020). The effects of the physical environment design on teachers' workplace comfort: A critical review. *The International Journal of Architectonic, Spatial, and Environmental Design, 14*(3), 17–30. https://doi.org/10.18848/2325-1662/cgp/v14i03/17-30

Baker, T. L., Wise, J., Kelley, G., & Skiba, R. J. (2016). Identifying barriers: Creating solutions to improve family engagement. *School Community Journal, 26*(2), 161–184.

Balban, M. Y., Neri, E., Kogon, M. M., Weed, L., Nouriani, B., Jo, B., Holl, G., Zeitzer, J. M., Spiegel, D., & Huberman, A. D. (2023). Brief structured respiration practices enhance mood and reduce physiological arousal. *Cell Reports Medicine, 4*(1), 100895. https://doi.org/10.1016/j.xcrm.2022.100895

Barker, S. (2019). *Mental wellbeing and psychology: The role of art and history in self-discovery and creation* (1st ed.). Routledge.

Bath, H. (2008). The three pillars of trauma-informed care. *Reclaiming Children and Youth, 17*(3), 17–21.

Beloglovsky, M. (2023). *Just play: Inspiring adult play in early childhood education.* Redleaf Press.

Bodell, L. (2022, March 28). Most change initiatives fail—Here's how to beat the odds. *Forbes.* https://www.forbes.com/sites/lisabodell/2022/03/28/most-change-initiatives-fail---heres-how-to-beat-the-odds/

Brainy Quote (n.d.). *Lynn Good Quotes.* Retrieved July 27, 2025, from https://www.brainyquote.com/quotes/lynn_good_790402

Brown, B. (2021). *Atlas of the heart: Mapping meaningful connection and the language of human experience.* Random House.

Brown, S., & Vaughan, C. (2009). *Play: How it shapes the brain, opens the imagination, and invigorates the soul.* Avery.

Buettner, C. K., Jeon, L., Hur, E., & Garcia, R. E. (2016). Teachers' social–emotional capacity: Factors associated with teachers' responsiveness and professional commitment. *Early Education and Development, 27*(7), 1018–1039. https://doi.org/10.1080/10409289.2016.1168227

Byington, T. A. (2023). *Find the joyful leader within: Banishing burnout in early childhood education.* Gryphon House, Inc.

Cacouris, C. (2022, January 5). Is looking at art a path to mental well-being? *WSJ: The Magazine from the Wall Street Journal.* https://www.wsj.com/health/wellness/art-mental-health-11641387911

Cambridge Dictionary. (n.d.). Confidence. In *Cambridge Dictionary.* Retrieved June 3, 2025, from https://dictionary.cambridge.org/dictionary/english/confidence

Cherry, K. (2025). *How to be open-minded and why it matters.* Verywell Mind. Retrieved September 19, 2025, from https://www.verywellmind.com/be-more-open-minded-4690673

Choi, G., & Bigelow, K. (2024). *Practitioner brief: culturally responsive practices to collaborate with families.* National Center for Pyramid Model Innovations

The Company Agency Leadership Council, Chernyshenko, D., Davies, S., Deighton, P., Fleurot, O., Frost, D., Gent, S. C., Glendinning, E., Jephson, M. J. J., Kirk, M., Kirsten, A. S.,

Tillman, H., & Younger, R. (2009). *Seven types of confidence.* The Company Agency. http://leadershipcouncil.co.uk/wp-content/uploads/2020/06/3-Seven_Types_of_confidence.pdf
Compassion Fatigue Awareness Project. (2017). *Recognizing compassion fatigue.* Accessed November 25, 2023, from www.compassionfatigue.org/pages/symptoms.html.
Dwyer, S. C., & Buckle, J. L. (2009). The space between: On being an insider-outsider in qualitative research. *International Journal of Qualitative Methods, 8*(1), 54–63.
Epstein, J. L. (2009). *School, family, and community partnerships: Your handbook for action.* Corwin Press.
Erdman, S., Colker, L. J., & Winter, E. C. (2020). *Trauma & young children: Teaching strategies to support & empower.* National Association for the Education of Young Children.
Ewenstein, B., Smith, W., & Sologar, A. (2015). *Changing change management.* McKinsey & Company. https://www.mckinsey.com/featured-insights/leadership/changing-change-management
Fehr, R., Fulmer, C. A., Awtrey, E. C., & Miller, J. A. (2017). The grateful workplace: A multilevel model of gratitude in organizations. *Academy of Management Review, 42*(2), 361–381.
Fisher, H. (2019, January 2). Chris Singleton believes love is greater than hate. *Charleston Living Magazine.* https://charlestonlivingmag.com/love-is-stronger-than-hate
Fox, E. G., Purtell, K. M., & Lang, S. N. (2025). *Exploring potential factors driving high turnover among early care and education teachers.* Crane Center for Early Childhood Research and Policy, The Ohio State University.
Fox, L., & Swett, J. (2017). *Concepts and strategies for families and schools in key context.* Center for Positive Behavioral Interventions and Supports.
Fredrickson, B. L. (2004). The broaden-and-build theory of positive emotions. *Philosophical Transactions of the Royal Science B: Biological Sciences, 359,* 1367–1377. http://dx.doi.org/10.1098/rstb.2004.1512
Friedman, S., & Mwenelupembe, A. (2020). *Each & every child: Teaching preschool with an equity lens.* National Association for the Education of Young Children.
Goldstein, D. (2022). Why you can't find child care: 100,000 workers are missing. *The New York Times.* https://www.nytimes.com/2022/10/13/us/child-care-worker-shortage.html
Goleman, D. (2006). *Emotional intelligence: Why it can matter more than IQ.* Bantam Books.
Gordon, J. (2017). *The power of positive leadership: How and why positive leaders transform teams and organizations and change the world.* John Wiley & Sons.
Gordon, J. (2007). *The energy bus: 10 rules to fuel your life, work, and team with positive energy.* John Wiley & Sons.
Grant, A. M. [@AdamMGrant]. (2022, January 14). *It's hard to keep an open mind if you don't have an open heart...* [Tweet]. Twitter. Retrieved March 25, 2025, from https://x.com/AdamMGrant/status/1482019030387068932
Grzybowski, J., & Brinthaupt, T. M. (2022). Trait mindfulness, self-compassion, and self-talk: A correlational analysis of young adults. *Behavioral Sciences, 12*(9), 300. https://doi.org/10.3390/bs12090300
Guitard, P., Ferland, F., & Ductil, E. (2024). Adult play and playfulness: A qualitative exploration of its meaning and importance for well-being. *Journal of Play in Adulthood, 2*(1), 1–20.
Hanh, T. N. (1991). *Peace is every step: The path of mindfulness in everyday life.* Bantam Books.
Holmes, T. H., & Rahe, R. H. (1967). The social readjustment rating scale. *Journal of Psychosomatic Research, 11*(2), 213–218.
Horton, C. B., Adam, H., & Galinsky, A. D. (2023). Evaluating the evidence for enclothed cognition: Z-curve and meta-analyses. *Personality and Social Psychology Bulletin.* https://doi.org/10.1177/01461672231182478
Hubel, G. S., Davies, F., Goodrum, N. M., Schmarder, K. M., Schnake, K., & Moreland, A. D. (2020). Adverse childhood experiences among early care and education teachers: Prevalence and associations with observed quality of classroom social and emotional climate. *Child & Youth Services Review, 111,* Article 104877.
Hylton, N. R., & Vu, J. A. (2019). Creating a work environment that supports staff retention. *Young Children, 74*(4), 34–38.
Jeffrey, J. K., Jackson Preston, P., Sanchez, D., & Herman, A. (2022). Organizational trauma-informed readiness, burnout and secondary traumatic stress among head start staff and educators during COVID-19. *Journal of Community Medicine & Public Health, 6*(3). https://doi.org/10.29011/2577-2228.100265
Jo, H., & Shin, D. (2025). The impact of recognition, fairness, and leadership on employee outcomes: A large-scale multi-group analysis. *PLOS One, 20*(1), Article e0312951.

Kaiser Permanente Oregon Educators Benefit Board. (2024, February 13). *Well-being spaces for teachers and staff.* Thriving Schools. https://thrivingschools.kaiserpermanente.org/labor-management-collaboration/well-being-spaces-for-teachers-and-staff/

Kanold, T. D., & Boogren, T. (2022). *Educator wellness: A guide for sustaining physical, mental, emotional, and social well-being.* Solution Tree Press.

Katz, L. G. (1972). Developmental stages of preschool teachers. *The Elementary School Journal, 73*(1), 50–54. https://doi.org/10.1086/460731

Kennedy, A., & Stonehouse, A. (2017). *Practice principle guide. Reflective practice.* Victorian Early Years Learning and Development Framework. https://www.education.vic.gov.au/Documents/childhood/providers/edcare/pracguidereflectivepractice2017.pdf

King, K. (2021, November 26) What does it mean to be trauma-informed. *Psychology Today.* https://www.psychologytoday.com/us/blog/lifespan-perspectives/202111/what-does-it-mean-be-trauma-informed?msockid=3a60dd2798006f9434bacedd99ee6e8a

Knoche, L. L., & Witte, A. L. (2016). Strengths-based educational interventions in rural settings: Promoting child development through home–school partnerships. In L. Crockett & G. Carlo (Eds), *Rural Ethnic Minority Youth and Families in the United States. Advancing Responsible Adolescent Development* (pp. 227–246). Springer. https://doi.org/10.1007/978-3-319-20976-0_13

Kokoros, T. (2023, April 19). *Why comfortable places to sit and a nice break room are important for early childhood educators.* Ideas and Innovations in Early Childhood Education. https://www.earlychildhoodeducationandcare.com/bloggers/2023/4/19/why-comfortable-places-to-sit-and-a-nice-break-room-are-important-for-early-childhood-educators

Koralek, D., Nemeth, K., & Ramsey, K. (2019). *Families & Educators together.* NAEYC.

Kottler, J. A., & Kottler, E. (2015). *Counseling skills for teachers* (reissue). Skyhorse Publishing.

Kriescher, S. L., Hulac, D. M., Ryan, A. M., & King, B. L. (2022). Evaluating the evidence for fidget toys in the classroom. *Intervention in School and Clinic, 59*(1), 66–69. https://doi.org/10.1177/10534512221130070

Krockow, E. M. (2019). Outsmart the anchoring bias in three simple steps. Psychological insights can help you avoid the trap of cognitive biases. *Psychology Today.* Retrieved October, 14, 2025 from https://www.psychologytoday.com/us/blog/stretching-theory/201902/outsmart-the-anchoring-bias-in-three-simple-steps

Krosofsky, A. (2020, December 15). *Why is gardening important? It has endless benefits for our health and environment.* Green Matters. https://www.greenmatters.com/p/why-gardening-is-important

Law, M., Karulkar, N., & Broadbent, E. (2021). Evidence for the effects of viewing visual artworks on stress outcomes: A scoping review. *BMJ Open, 11*(6). https://doi.org/10.1136/bmjopen-2020-043549

Lee, I. F. (2018a). *Joyful: The surprising power of ordinary things to create extraordinary happiness.* Little Brown Spark.

Lee, I. F. (2018b, April). *Where joy hides and how to find it* [Video]. Ted Conferences. https://www.ted.com/talks/ingrid_fetell_lee_where_joy_hides_and_how_to_find_it

Leung, M., Chan, J. K. W., & Wang, Z. (2006). Impact of school facilities on working behavior of teachers. *International Journal of Strategic Property Management, 10*(2), 79–91. https://doi.org/10.3846/1648715x.2006.9637546

Lewis, H. R., Lipscomb, S. T., Hatfield, B. E., Weber, R., Green, B., & Patterson, L. (2023). Family–teacher relationships and child engagement in early care and education. *Societies, 13*(3), 67. https://doi.org/10.3390/soc13030067

Longfellow, H. W. (n.d.). Kind hearts are the gardens . . . [Quote]. AZQuotes. Retrieved August 23, 2025, from https://www.azquotes.com/quote/509639

Luciw, L. (2023). Mitigating the impacts of secondary trauma in K–12 educators. *Canadian Journal for New Scholars in Education, 14*(1), 1–16

Marx-Mackerley, R., Byington, T. A., Wright, S. E., & Peshlakai, C. L. (2021). *Making space for preschool makerspaces.* Gryphon House.

Merriam-Webster. (n.d.). Encourage. In *Merriam-Webster.com dictionary.* Retrieved December 8, 2025, from https://www.merriam-webster.com/dictionary/encourage

Merriam-Webster. (n.d.). Manage. In *Merriam-Webster.com dictionary.* Retrieved August 6, 2025, from https://www.merriam-webster.com/dictionary/manage

Mu, F., Liu, J., Lou, H., Zhu, W., Wang, Z., & Li, B. (2024). How breaking a sweat affects mood: The mediating role of self-efficacy between physical exercise and emotion regulation ability. *PLOS One, 19*(6), Article 0303694. https://doi.org/10.1371/journal.pone.0303694

NAEYC. (2020). *DAP: Creating a caring, equitable community of learners*. NAEYC. www.naeyc.org. https://www.naeyc.org/resources/position-statements/dap/creating-community

Neff, K. (2011). *Self-compassion: The proven power of being kind to yourself.* William Morrow.

Neff, K. D., Knox, M. C., Long, P., & Gregory, K. (2020). Caring for others without losing yourself: An adaptation of the Mindful Self-Compassion Program for Healthcare Communities. *Journal of Clinical Psychology, 76*(9), 1543–1562. https://doi.org/10.1002/jclp.23007

Nikolopoulos, K. (2025). *What is anchoring bias. Definition & examples.* Scribbr. Retrieved March 30, 2026, from https://www.scribbr.com/research-bias/anchoring-bias/

Oxford Dictionary (n.d.). Encourage. In *Oxford dictionary.* OxfordLearnersDictionaries.com

Patrick, P., Reupert, A., Berger, E., Morris, Z., Diamond, Z., Hammer, M., Hine, R., & Fathers, C. (2024). Initiatives for promoting educator wellbeing: A Delphi study. *BMC Psychology, 12,* Article 220.

Pollack, J. (2025, May 28). *Dealing with difficult teachers as a school administrator or principal.* Peaceful Leaders Academy.

Portis, A. (2006). *Not a box.* Houghton Mifflin Harcourt.

Price, C. (2021). *The power of fun: How to feel alive again.* The Dial Press.

Prince, A. J., & Roca, F. (2005). *Twenty-one elephants and still standing.* Houghton Mifflin.

Proyer, R. T., & Brauer, K. (2024a). How does playfulness (re)frame the world? Evidence for selective processing advantages in visual attention. *Frontiers in Psychology, 14,* Article 1462980.

Proyer, R. T., & Brauer, K. (2024b). Correlates of self- and peer-rated playfulness and coping strategies. *Journal of Leisure Research, 55*(2), 211–237.

Rieth, C. (2023). Empowered circles: using talking circles in research. *New England College Journal of Applied Educational Research, 4,* 1–23. https://files.eric.ed.gov/fulltext/EJ1431787.pdf

Rosenow, N. (2023). *Encouragement every day.* Exchange Press.

Schaack, D. D., Le, V.-N., & Stedron, J. (2020). When fulfillment is not enough: Early childhood teacher occupational burnout and turnover intentions from a job demands and resources perspective. *Early Education and Development, 31*(7), 1011–1030. https://doi.org/10.1080/10409289.2020.1791648

Schein, E. H. (2010). *Organizational culture and leadership.* Jossey-Bass.

Shapiro, J. (2024, November 12). How leaders can positively energize and encourage others. *Psychology Today.* https://www.psychologytoday.com/us/blog/well-being-is-foundational-of-leadership/202411/how-leaders-can-positively-energize-and

Sheridan, S. M., & Kim, E. M. (2015). *Processes and pathways of family-school partnerships across development.* Springer.

Simpson, C. (2025). Why change management fails: It's about people, not process. *Forbes.* https://www.forbes.com/sites/forbesbooksauthors/2025/05/06/why-change-management-fails-its-about-people-not-process/

Substance Abuse and Mental Health Services Administration, SAMHSA. (2024). *Trauma and violence.* SAMHSA. https://www.samhsa.gov/mental-health/trauma-violence

Tschannen-Moran, M. (2014). *Trust matters: Leadership for successful schools.* Jossey-Bass.

Untitled Leader. (2024). *Rise to lead: Transforming teams through uplifting leadership.* https://www.untitledleader.com/leadership/rise-to-lead-transforming-teams-through-uplifting-leadership/

Vance, N. (2024). Joyce Epstein's school-family-community partnership model. In *EBSCO Research Starters.* https://www.ebsco.com/research-starters/education/joyce-epsteins-school-family-community-partnership-model

Vanheems, B. (2025). *Companion planting chart and guide for vegetable gardens.* Almanac.com. https://www.almanac.com/companion-planting-guide-vegetables

Villalobos, J. P., Valverde, P. A., & Farewell, C. V. (2024). Exploring the perceptions and cultural differences surrounding mindfulness among early childhood education informal caregivers: A qualitative study. *Journal of Education and Health Promotion, 13*(1). https://doi.org/10.4103/jehp.jehp_181_24

Walker, T. (2019, October 18). *"I didn't know it had a name": Secondary traumatic stress and educators.* NEA Today. Retrieved November 4, 2025, from https://www.nea.org/nea-today/all-news-articles/i-didnt-know-it-had-name-secondary-traumatic-stress-and-educators.

Waters, L. E., Loton, D., & Jach, H. K. (2018). Does strength-based parenting predict academic achievement? The mediating effects of perseverance and engagement. *Journal of Happiness Studies, 20*(4), 1121–1140. https://doi.org/10.1007/s10902-018-9983-1

Index

Note: Page numbers followed by *f*, *t*, and indicate figures and tables, respectively.